MY DAD'S CLASS

AN INTENTIONAL STRUCTURE FOR
TEACHING KIDS ABOUT MONEY AND LIFE

MY

DAD'S

CLASS

PAIGE CORNETET

LIONCREST
PUBLISHING

Copyright © 2022 Paige Cornetet

MY DAD'S CLASS

An Intentional Structure for Teaching Kids About Money and Life

ISBN 978-1-5445-2457-3 Hardcover
         978-1-5445-2455-9 Paperback
         978-1-5445-2456-6 Ebook

For Mom

CONTENTS

INTRODUCTION

In the spring of 2020, I felt a lot like a princess locked in a tower.

Like everyone else, I had been placed under the curse of the pandemic, and I was trapped at home. In this story, Rapunzel wears pajama pants and a messy bun while she tries out some new internet recipes and putters around her apartment, looking for anything besides cable news to fill the long days. I had just gotten married in January, so I wasn't waiting for a prince—he was already in the room next door, murmuring about force majeure on Zoom calls with the other housebound lawyers in his firm.

It's hardly a castle, so while he's working I sit in my little corner of the living room / kitchen. I sit on my purple bouncy ball, using my iMac like a magic mirror to the outside world.

I am so, so bored.

But I am also hard at work growing a human. No one but my husband, Peter, can see me as my baby bump grows, but it's happening all the same. As I round into what should be the fun part of my pregnancy with cute maternity clothes and lots of compliments about my pregnant-lady glow, it suddenly hits me:

I have come full circle.

I was a child and now I am a parent. I'm embarking on the next phase of my life—the part where I'm responsible for teaching my children everything they'll need to know to become successful adults.

So how do I do that? What kind of mom do I want to be, and how do I make sure I teach my kids all the values and habits I want them to know? Before the pandemic, I was busy running around traveling, fluttering into the next event, party, or trip without much room to breathe. But with three months of being locked in, I had time to think about exactly what was important to me with raising kids.

For me, the easiest way to move forward into the future was to go backward. I spent a lot of lockdown looking back on my childhood and remembering what my parents taught me. I actually have notes on the subject, because every Saturday my dad sat me and my siblings down for Dad's Class, which was a series of lessons about money management, the world of work, and the family business. He left nothing to chance when it came to the lessons he wanted us to learn, and it's all right there in the spiral-bound notebooks I wrote in each weekend.

As I looked back, I also saw that Dad's Class was the culmination of my parents' very intentional thinking about how they wanted to raise us. These weren't just money lessons, but life lessons.

And if they could do it for me, I could do it for my own children, too.

YOUR CHILDREN WILL LEARN, WHETHER YOU TEACH THEM OR NOT

In our fast-paced world, parents are *busy*. We work hard, we travel, we go to church and volunteer. And on top of all that, we want to give our children everything they need to thrive. That starts with the basics of food and shelter, but it also extends into the future and how to make sure our children can eventually provide those things for themselves.

This is the big question that all parents have: How do we make sure we teach our children everything they need to know to thrive. We all have our own specific version of this problem. For my dad, the question was, How do I run a company and raise four kids in a way that lets me be present with them and teach them life lessons?

That's a tall order, and while I was thinking about my own transition into parenthood, I realized that *all* parents are wrestling with the same issue. How can you be absolutely sure you're preparing your kids for life in the real world, where money can be tight and the pressure is high?

Depending on your situation—including how you were raised, your current financial outlook, and your personal values—you might be asking yourself several different versions of that big question:

- How do I teach my kids about money concepts?

- How do I make sure they understand the basics of saving and investing?

- At what age do I start teaching my kids, and when are they old enough to get it?

- How do I make sure my kids don't end up becoming entitled, spoiled brats?

That last one is probably the biggest question of all, especially for parents who are able to provide extras, like piano lessons, summer camp, and maybe even private school. When you're giving them so much, how can you also make sure your kids understand the value of what they've received?

Many of these questions tap into anxieties we have around money. If you didn't have a solid financial education yourself, you may not know where to start in teaching your own children about personal finance. But here's the thing: Your children will learn about money from you no matter what. They will watch your behavior and take in every word of your conversations about money, spending and saving. They will absorb your attitudes and your actions, and because personal finance isn't taught in school, you will be your child's main teacher on the subject—even if you never say a direct word about it.

PARENTING WITH INTENTION

The solution to the problem of teaching children about money is to become very intentional about providing a financial education. Your children will learn money lessons from you no matter what, so why not be intentional about what you want to teach? It's within your power to choose what they learn about money, and you can start very, very early.

Of course, the road to hell is paved with good intentions, so parents need more than just the desire to help their kids learn about money. They need a *structure*. This is where my dad excelled as a businessman and as a parent: he was very good at creating structures that kept our family organized and made sure his household was run in a way that let us live out our family values. My Dad's

Class is the embodiment of this intentional structure, and it's a solution that any family can take and adapt to meet their own needs.

WHAT YOU'LL LEARN FROM MY DAD'S CLASS

This book is meant to be a practical guide for creating structure and consistency in your family so that you make money lessons an integral part of your children's lives. Effective financial education isn't accomplished with a one-off lesson about passbook savings at age ten and a single talk about credit cards before leaving for college. To help your child internalize the value of a dollar—and your family values, too—you need to provide regular opportunities to learn and practice.

This book will show you how to accomplish that by making money lessons a regular part of your family life and putting them squarely in the context of the larger life lessons you wish to impart. Specifically, you'll learn to:

- Articulate your family values so that your children can not only learn them, but live them

- Create family rules and a structure for fostering personal accountability

- Embed your values into daily routines and special family traditions

- Establish a family economy to teach the basics of saving and spending

- Start a family bank to teach the power of investing

- Develop your own Mom or Dad's Class to share your skills and passions

- Leverage your community to provide additional lessons about work and personal finance

I'll also share stories and examples from my Dad's Class to show you how these lessons worked in my life. Each chapter will also provide plenty of practical advice to help you explore your own values and hopefully inspire you to make my Dad's Class into your own intentional structure for teaching your children with your own lesson content.

WHY I WROTE THIS BOOK

I've always been passionate about empowering kids to take charge of their money. My first books I wrote were for children, and the "Spend-Then" series explores the importance of saving and planning for the future in a fun, kid-friendly way.

I also run a business called Millennial Guru that helps people transform their talents into workplace strengths and to understand how to work with team members who have very different strengths. The throughline in my work is that I've always been passionate about helping people better understand themselves, then to harness that knowledge and turn it into action.

As I reflected on my personal transition from child to parent during the pandemic, I realized that I could take my core skills and use them to help parents become better financial teachers for their children. In this book, I want to help parents understand themselves and what they value and provide them with a useful structure for teaching their children about money.

And I am living proof that this type of intentional teaching works. I've been a student in my Dad's Class, and it gave me the confidence not only to manage my money well, but to tackle all sorts of challenges in life, including starting my own business. These lessons were the foundations for my whole life, and now I'm ready to teach them myself. My parents did it, and you and I can do it for our own children too.

Though the baby I carried while I was locked in my tower didn't live to see the world open back up again, I still became a parent when he was born early that spring. Completing the transition from child to parent was a blessing that opened up my eyes and heart to the importance of being my child's first and best teacher about life. I know now that I can do it.

Deep down, I've always known that I can do it, because that was one of the very first lessons my dad instilled in us with a set of family mottoes that we recited every night. So let's start with those mottoes and how to create them.

1

CREATE "OUT-LOUD"
FAMILY SAYINGS

For as far back as I can remember, my family had a special nighttime routine. After dinner and bathtime, as we were winding down and getting ready for bed, my younger sister Brooke and I—and later, my sister Claire and brother Peter—would meet my dad in the hallway behind the kitchen for out-loud family sayings.

This was not a fancy part of our house. It was just the hallway that led from the garage to the kitchen, a boring pass-through that most people wouldn't spend much time in at all. But my dad turned this spot into a central part of my childhood—and a touchstone that would influence me for my entire adult life.

So here we stood, two little girls who hadn't quite even learned to read yet, me in my Princess Jasmine nightgown and Brooke in her red footie pajamas. There in the hallway, at kid-height, was a poster of our family sayings. We would stand together each night with my dad, who would read each saying aloud to us.

"I can do it," he prompted.

"I can do it!" Brooke and I called out in unison. As we said our part, we would jump up together like we were doing a jumping jack. We'd land with our arms and legs spread wide to create a star shape with our bodies to reinforce the message that we were superstars who really could do anything we set our minds to.

We did this just about every evening, no matter what was going on in the world or in our lives. So it's no wonder that I can still say them now, exactly as they were written on that old piece of posterboard in the hallway. Even before I could read the words on my own, I knew them:

I can do it.

Do what's right.

Do your best.

Treat other people how you want to be treated—nice.

There, in big, bold script, was everything my dad wanted us to know about life. It wasn't anything fancy, and today I can look back and smile at how they weren't perfect. My dad obviously wasn't a great grammarian and had just added the word "nice" to the end of his thought to drive the point home, but we learned it all the same. Ask any of my siblings today about our out-loud family sayings, and they can recite them back to you. That's how chiseled into our minds they are.

And yet, nothing about out-loud family sayings was boring or difficult. This wasn't one of those things you had to memorize under orders in school, like the times tables or the preamble to the Constitution. What I remember most was that it all felt really *fun*.

As we got older, my dad began building conversations around our family sayings. When it was time for me to go to kindergarten for the first time, I know we spent more time on exactly what "I can do it" meant. And after any big event, whether it was a dance recital or a big test, the follow-up question was always, "Well, did you do your best? Did you give it your all?"

And so we learned our out-loud family sayings first, and eventually we began to talk about how they could be put into action in our daily lives. This routine became such a big part of our childhood that even my friend Rachel knew the sayings by heart. She would come over to play and stay for dinner, and she would get roped into saying them with us. This was a daily commitment, and it didn't matter if we had guests.

But my dad always made sure out-loud family sayings were fun, so it was never a problem to include a friend. It's a testament to the power of this routine—the repetition, the kid-friendly wording and motions, the personalized discussions—that we all grew up with four "rules" for living that were etched in our hearts and that we could fall back on in any situation.

Out-loud family sayings were the foundation of my dad's very intentional teaching and parenting, and they'll form the basis of how I approach parenting my own children in the future.

And they can work for your family, too.

CREATING AND USING OUT-LOUD FAMILY SAYINGS

Out-loud family sayings are, at their heart, your family values put into words. Done right, these are powerful statements that will stick with kids for life and empower them to act in ways that will be productive and help them be their best selves.

In the business world, this would be the mission statement that sums up a company's vision and beliefs. But if you've ever clicked through to a mission statement from an "About Us" page on a company's website, you know that those words often end up being pretty vague. They can leave you with the sense that you just read something meaningful, but you'd be hard-pressed to actually put your finger on what it was.

Out-loud family sayings are designed specifically for kids, so you can skip the fancy corporate speak and go straight for the simplest, most kid-friendly language to encapsulate the idea. The out-loud family sayings my dad designed are burned into my memory—and possibly even the memories of my friends and neighbors—so what he did definitely worked. From my vantage point as an adult, I can see that there are a few key components that make out-loud sayings work:

- Broad values that can be applied in many situations.

- Short, kid-friendly phrases that focus on action.

- No more than five sayings to memorize.

- Multisensory input.

- Daily repetition.

- Ongoing discussion.

From the moment he became a father, my dad was intentional about wanting to be part of his children's lives, not just as a distant provider, but as an active manager of how we were raised. He embraced the work of being a parent. His strong sense of what it meant to raise competent children came directly through his experiences working in the family business side by side with his grandfather and receiving a truly multigenerational education. In his own reading and learning, Dad took notes and distilled what he had read into a simple phrase to memorize and share, so it was natural for him to do the same with his personal values. Our original out-loud sayings were:

I can do it.

Do what's right.

Do your best.

Treat other people how you want to be treated—nice.

Each one of these encapsulates a broad value into easy, age-appropriate language. For example, "I can do it" imparts the value of personal responsibility and the importance of hard work, while instilling self-confidence. That's a lot for a four-word sentence! But unlike a corporate mission statement that would look for the fanciest phrases to get those ideas across, a good out-loud family saying does it simply.

My dad also recognized that he didn't have to try to put every possible contingency into his out-loud sayings. For example, "Do what's right" very clearly references right versus. wrong, but it's flexible enough to apply to any situation. Whether it's a question of sneaking a cookie before dinner or making choices about tricky office politics, the out-loud saying is a reminder to turn to your family values when they're most needed. They can be used in any context, which lets them grow right along with your child.

Out-loud family sayings also have a lot of energy and action behind them. Every one of them has the word "do" in it, because just talking about values isn't the point—it's about acting on them. (Actually, the last one uses the word "treat" instead of "do," but look closely and you'll see it's a riff on the Golden Rule's "Do unto others" language, so I think it counts!) Out-loud sayings are the words that represent how you go about your family life together.

Once my dad put his values into words, he also led us to put them into action. This started with putting the words on the poster so that we could have visual input to read as we heard them and then said them out loud. We also added some physical actions when we said the phrases. This extra step involved our whole bodies in the learning process and made the words even more memorable and meaningful. It also made out-loud family sayings a lot of fun!

Crucially, out-loud family sayings were more than just a family motto that Dad hung on the wall and we glanced at on our way to school. Instead, he would lead us back to the out-loud sayings on a daily basis. We said them out loud—a *lot*. He also turned the out-loud sayings into a continuous conversation: we looked at them, discussed them, and talked about them in a whole range of situations. Any time a situation got hard, we were directed back to our out-loud family sayings as the jumping off point to work through the problem.

When I was younger, I loved to be on stage. I did a lot of theater, and even though I loved it, there was always that moment right before going on when a wave of stage fright would wash over me. I remember when I was about ten or so, I started to feel jittery waiting for my cue, and I just took a deep breath and said to myself "I can do it. I am going to do my best." It was at this moment that those words I had been repeating for as long as I could remember just came to me, and their meaning was suddenly crystal clear. I knew I *could* do it. I knew I would get out there and do my best, and if I messed up, it would be okay, because I was going to give it my all. This is when the words transformed from just a fun bedtime activity to something I knew I could rely on in my life.

That realization wasn't some kind of magical bolt from the blue, though. My dad had already paved the way for it to happen when he would guide us through our problems by going back to the sayings. Any time one of us was scared or struggling with something, he walked us over to the poster and had us repeat the sayings. Then we'd talk about how they could apply to our problems. This intentional practice made it possible for me not only to memorize the phrases but gradually to be able to apply them on my own, too.

Even today, I still find myself turning to an out-loud family saying when I need help working through a challenge. I'm thirty-one years old, and I'll often ask myself if I'm doing what's right. It's a touchstone that I reach for when I'm making decisions and seeking to understand other people's perspectives. I may not always have the answer, but my parents taught me how important it was to ask the question and to do my best to do what's right. That's the gift of the out-loud family saying: it's a value that you take with you forever.

WHY OUT-LOUD FAMILY SAYINGS ARE IMPORTANT

Out-loud family sayings are the foundation for everything you'll teach your children as they grow. Think of them as the ABCs of your framework for teaching values. A child can't learn to read without first knowing all the letters and the sounds they make, so from the time they're old enough to sing along, we're getting kids to sing their ABCs and point out letters of the alphabet in everyday life. Someday your kids will be reading chapter books and writing research papers, but they'll never get there without the fundamentals of language.

Out-loud family sayings are the fundamentals for life learning. Someday you want your children to be able to make good decisions about money, life, and relationships, but you start with the basics. For my dad, those basics were values about working hard, doing what's right, and treating others well. You'll be able to layer in a lot of lessons that go back to those basics as your kids get older, but you want to start early—ideally, as soon as your kids are old enough to talk. By age three, you can start instilling your most basic values by having your kids repeat them back to you. Financial independence, self-reliance, and independent thinking all start here.

We'll talk more about developing the all-important content of your sayings in the next section, but it's also worth exploring why the method behind them is so effective. My parents were big believers in the Montessori method of teaching—so much so, in fact, that my dad wanted to tear out our bathroom and remodel the house to have child-sized fixtures to support this method of learning.

Maria Montessori was an influential educator who developed a system of early childhood teaching that puts the child at the center of learning. A Montessori classroom is designed with a child in mind, so furniture and materials are all kid-sized and easy to use. Learning is an act of exploration, and students are given many opportunities to practice and repeat activities at their own pace until they have achieved mastery.[1] The Montessori method is also based on a multisensory approach that lives by the mantra: "Never give more to the eye and the ear than you do to the hand."[2]

My parents were all-in on the Montessori method, and they both understood just how important it would be to raise kids who could be self-starters and take charge of their own learning. For my dad, that came from his experience in business, working with a range of different people and having to understand their styles and how to get the best out of them. My parents also had four children, and it was clear to them that we were all very different, from our talents to our learning styles.

For example, I was a performer who loved to be on stage, but Brooke hated going to ballet class—except for the end, when she could spend her money on the candy machine in the lobby. My youngest sister Claire is a talented artist, while my brother has this steel-trap of a memory that lets him quote movies and the tiniest details of information. We all have different strengths, and my parents realized early on that what worked for teaching one child might not work for the others.

---

[1] "The Montessori Method," Fundación Argentina María Montessori, accessed May 19, 2021, https://www.fundacionmontessori.org/the-montessori-method.htm.

[2] Fawn Ventura, "Sensorial Development in Montessori Education," Amity Montessori, September 28, 2020, https://www.amitymontessori.com/blog/sensorial-development-in-montessori-education/.

Taking a multisensory approach to out-loud family sayings makes sure that everyone can access the lesson and learn it in their own way. For my brother, hearing the words was probably enough, while I got more from acting out the motions that went with each saying. As a parent of very young children, you might not yet even know which learning style works best for your child. It can take years to discover this! In the meantime, it makes sense to provide as many ways as possible to absorb the information through a multisensory approach. Visual aids, stories, songs, motions—the more ways you can provide as you repeat the out-loud daily sayings, the more easily your child will retain the information. It will also make out-loud family sayings lots of fun!

In addition to setting up out-loud family sayings to be kid-friendly and multisensory, my dad was also willing to commit to a lot of repetition. It couldn't have been all that interesting for him to repeat the same sayings every single night before bed, but repetition is the key to learning—especially for young children.

For children, repetition is not just doing the same thing twice. For adults, it's easy to get tired of watching *Frozen* over and over or reading the same bedtime story every night. It's totally natural to cringe a little inside when a toddler claps and says, "Again! Again!"

But children learn something different every time they repeat the experience of that story.[3] For them, it is new each time. For example, you could be reading a book to a one-year-old, and the first fifty times they're just trying to absorb the story. First it might be the pictures, then starting to connect the words they hear to the images they see. Later, they'll begin to connect the words on the page to the words you're saying, and still other times they might repeat the words along with you, sometimes focusing on how it sounds and others on how it feels to form the syllables with their mouths.

You might be totally over *The Little Engine That Could*, but for a kid, it's very literally never the same thing twice.

If you're still a little skeptical about just how much repetition children need, consider just how much information is coming at a child on a daily basis. When you start a new storybook, every part of it is a novel experience, from its size and shape to the story and pictures, and even the voices you choose to give to different characters when you read it aloud.

For adults, novelty is exciting, but for kids, it can be stressful. That's because they are actually burning energy as their brains

---

[3] Matt Arnerich, "Play. Learn. Repeat. The Power of Repetition in the Early Years," Famly, June 27, 2018, accessed May 19, 2021, https://www.famly.co/blog/play-learn-repeat-repetition-early-years.

build new neurological connections.[4] With each new bit of information, they are working to figure out what it means and sort it into the right mental category for the future. The whole process of reading is automatic for you because you have had years to build those neural pathways. For children, it takes a lot of work. It explains why nap time is so inviting!

Given all the energy it takes to deal with so much incoming information, it's no wonder that the young search for understanding and predictability. Being able to predict what's coming—as they can on the hundredth time through a favorite movie, book, puzzle or building set—provides a sense of safety and security. And these are basic human needs. It's not just knowledge that grows, but also the feeling that "I know what this is. I am okay."

Looking back on my own childhood, what could feel more secure than being in my cozy pajamas, hanging out with my dad, and having a little more fun before bed? From the perspective of adulthood, I can see that out-loud family sayings gave me and my siblings a chance to relax at night after a long day of learning to navigate the world. In those moments, we got to feel completely comfortable as we went through our sayings together. It was a gift.

---

[4] "Repetition and Child Development in Montessori Education," Montessori Academy, May 4, 2017, https://montessoriacademy.com.au/repetition-child-development-montessori/.

Research also shows that repetition can help children develop a strong sense of self-worth.[5] Every time a child walks through an activity, their knowledge in how to do it becomes more secure and their feelings of mastery and self-worth increase.

For my parents, that was the whole intention behind out-loud family sayings. They wanted us to be independent and proud of ourselves. When it comes to raising self-confident, empowered kids, we should never underestimate the power of repetition: of our values, our lessons—and of the fun times, too.

HOW TO DEVELOP YOUR OWN OUT-LOUD FAMILY SAYINGS

The power of out-loud family sayings is that they take your vague, internal ideas about how you want to raise your kids and force you to get specific. You have to put your ideas into words, and then you put them out there to live by—for yourself and your kids.

So let's get intentional about putting these touchstone ideas into words.

---

[5] Matt Arnerich, "Play. Learn. Repeat. The Power of Repetition in the Early Years," Famly, June 27, 2018, https://www.famly.co/blog/play-learn-repeat-repetition-early-years.

Step One: Discover Your Personal Values

First, take the time to sit down and think about what you value most in life. These are big questions! Your answers don't have to be ready for publication, but you should take the time to think deeply and jot down some key phrases or bullet points that get at the heart of your ideas.

Answer these questions on your own first:

1. What does it mean to be a good person?

2. What does it mean to be a successful adult?

3. What personal traits do you most want to instill in your children? (For example: creativity, grit, kindness, ambition, charity, faith, confidence, competence, collaboration.)

4. What beliefs do you want to pass on to your children? (These could be faith-based, personally held, or tied to your family's intergenerational wisdom.)

Step Two: Come Together With Your Partner

If you're raising your children with a spouse or partner, you'll need to get on the same page about the values you want to pass on. Once your partner answers the questions above, it's time to sit down and compare notes. You might want to get a cup of coffee—this will be a deep discussion!

First, see what you have in common. If you both value hard work and respect for elders, great! Get out a fresh piece of paper and list all the values you agree are important for your family to live by.

Next, discuss the values that you didn't have in common. Does your partner actually agree with that value and just didn't think to list it? Or do you have real disagreements about what's important? Take the time to listen to each other and see if you can come to an agreement about whether or not a value belongs on your final list or not. Try not to treat this as a debate to win, though. You're on the same team, and you're working together to build a structure for your whole family. You'll need to come to consensus about what's most important for your children. You might end up rewording some values to work for both of you, or you may have to let some go. That's okay!

As you work your way through your different ideas, continue to add values you agree on to your list. At this point—or at any point!—you may need a break. That's okay too. Your family values and out-loud sayings are a work in progress, and nothing needs to be set in stone. If you get stuck, remember that you will be writing these on a ninety-nine-cent piece of posterboard, not carving them into stone tablets. You can always change or add to them later. Stay flexible!

Step Three: Choose 3-5 Actionable Values

Once you've completed your list of shared values, review them with your partner to see which ones are *actionable*. This is key. Your out-loud family sayings will be the foundation for teaching your kids to *do* the things you want them to do as adults—namely, to *live* your values, not just talk about them.

That means that each value will need to have an action verb tied to it. For example, suppose one of your shared values was faith. That's great! But how does it play out when verbalized by the family saying? Faith on its own is just a word, but what actions can you tie to it to make it come to life?

This may take another round of brainstorming to explore what aspects of faith are most important to you. Do you want your children to worship regularly? Thank God for their blessings? Treat others with compassion and respect? You may find that one of your values leads to several actionable out-loud family sayings—or you might find that a particular value doesn't really work as an out-loud family saying. This is fine! There's no right or wrong way to create your out-loud daily sayings. As long as each one is built around an action that reflects your values, you're on the right track.

Once you turn your values into sayings, review your list. Select three to five out-loud daily sayings that you like best. These will probably be the ones that are the easiest to say—remember, they're meant to be for kids!—and that cover the values you feel are most important.

Step Four: Teach Your Out-Loud Family Sayings

Now comes the fun part! Print your new out-loud family sayings on a poster and hang it where your kids can see it. Take a cue from Montessori education and hang it at eye level for your children in a place where they have plenty of space to move as they recite them with you.

Next, find a time every day when you can visit the poster with your kids. This could be before or after dinner, or just before bed. The exact timing isn't important, as long as you commit to building out-loud daily sayings into your daily routine. Have your kids repeat them every day, and add motions or dance moves to keep it fun.

Your whole family will have your out-loud family sayings memorized in no time, and that's when you can begin to refer to them to prompt better behavior and deeper problem-solving throughout their childhoods. When you know your values by heart, it's much easier to put them into action—a lifelong skill that starts *today*.

KEY TAKEAWAYS

Actionable Idea

Kid-Friendly

Repeat Daily

In this chapter, we learned how to turn your ideas about family values into actionable, easy-to-remember sayings that your children can memorize. Out-loud family sayings work best when they are kid-friendly, delivered in a multisensory way, and repeated daily. As your children grow, you'll be able to refer back to our out-loud family sayings to guide them in their decision-making, help them work through problems, and eventually live by your values as thriving, independent adults.

Young children are primed to learn, and they soak up everything they see and hear—especially the things they have repeated contact with. Your children are going to learn from you no matter what. They're always listening to you, even when you're not speaking directly to them. They're always watching you, even when you think they aren't paying attention. As a parent, you get to decide what your children absorb at home. Out-loud family sayings allow you to be intentional about what you choose to pass down to them.

My dad was very intentional about our out-loud family sayings, and while I'm no longer reciting the words in my PJs before bed, I still rely on these sayings at every major transition in my life.

When I was eighteen, I took a huge leap of faith to move to New York City for a month for an internship. It was scary to suddenly be thrown into the world of adulthood and have to learn how to get around one of the world's biggest cities—not to mention navigating roommate issues, learning how to cook, and managing a budget on my own. But the words "I can do it" always rang in my ears, and I had been saying them for so long that I truly believed them.

Did I do my best? Yes. Did I do what was right? These out-loud family sayings helped me transition successfully into adulthood—and "I can do it" gave me the confidence to make the leap. Four powerful little sentences helped make me the woman I am today, and as I start my own journey into marriage and parenthood, I can't wait to pass on my own out-loud family sayings to the next generation.

But it's not enough just to repeat your values each day. You also need to develop family rules and a useful structure that will allow everyone in your family to carry out those values in daily life.

2

LAY DOWN THE LAW

My sister Brooke and I are very close in age, so we were always getting into each other's things. By the time I was ten, I was sick of it. By then, I had three siblings, and I just wanted to have a few things for myself.

One day, I found out that Brooke had taken my favorite toy without asking. I can't remember what the toy even was anymore, but I definitely remember the feeling of frustration boiling over. This was the last straw, and I let her know it.

I grabbed that toy and bopped her over the head with it.

Now that we were in a full-blown fight, my dad stepped in. As soon as he entered the room, we knew what would happen. Now wasn't the time to plead our case. No adult was in the room to see what happened, and my dad wasn't about to negotiate with children about who did what.

So we dragged ourselves over to the repenting bench and prepared ourselves for a long, quiet sit.

In our house, the repenting bench was a hard, stone hearth that was raised from the floor. It was big enough for kids to sit on, and I'm sure my parents chose it because it was so uncomfortable. When you were sent to the repenting bench, you had to sit and think about what you had done until you were calmed down enough to talk it out with whoever got sent to the repenting bench with you. You couldn't leave the repenting bench until both parties agreed to confess to their role in the altercation and take their story together to the parent who sent them to the bench.

On this occasion, I was much angrier than Brooke because I felt somewhat justified in my righteous rage about her taking my stuff. I was prepared to sit there for quite some time nursing my grudge. But Brooke *hated* the repenting bench and would very quickly be ready to move on so she could go play.

That's when the negotiations started. "Come on, let's just talk to Dad," she said. "I don't care anymore and just want to go outside and play." I felt my power here, because I could keep Brooke on the bench by refusing to get up. Eventually she offered me a portion of her candy stash, and I relented. (To this day, I'm sure that my talents at the negotiating table came directly from these early experiences on the repenting bench!)

When we left the bench to find Dad, we each explained our side of the conflict. This wasn't about our parents serving as judge and jury to determine fault. In fact, the repenting bench rather brilliantly served as a neutral third party in that regard. By the time we were ready to talk, we had to show that we understood our own role in the dispute and accept responsibility for our own actions. In this case, Dad took the opportunity to ask if hitting Brooke—whether she stole my toy or not—was a good example of treating people nicely, as laid out in our out-loud family sayings. (It was not.)

Once the confession was over, we were each expected to apologize, promise not to do it again, hug it out, and move on.

And we did. Over and over, throughout our childhood, as we internalized both our family laws and the values behind them.

CREATING FAMILY LAWS FOR
STRUCTURE AND ACCOUNTABILITY

For my dad, creating a structure and maintaining order is a bedrock principle, in business and in life. Dad ran his business from our house, and he knew that he would not be able to make that a success if his workplace descended into chaos. He was very much of the opinion that "if my space is not clean, my mind is not clean."

Raising four kids could have been a recipe for disaster. We're talking about four small humans who liked to dance and sing. We played and screamed and ran around. Without structure and some very clear ground rules, my dad would not have been able to create the life he wanted for himself and for our family as a whole.

The solution, which my parents discovered in a wonderful book by Linda and Richard Eyre[6], was to create very clear family laws that were so simple to learn that we could be held accountable for living up to them from a very early age. These laws embodied my dad's desire for structure on a daily basis as well as my parents' deeply held Christian values about how to treat each other and what it means to be a good person.

And they did it in just five words:

- Peace

- Asking

- Order

---

[6] Linda and Richard Eyre, *Teaching Your Children Values* (New York: Simon and Schuster, 1993).

- Respect

- Obedience

It's important to note here that, while these rules were informed by my parents' values, they weren't meant to be values statements alone. They were *laws*. We were expected to live by them to make sure that our family life looked and felt the way my parents believed it should. Whenever one of us did something out of bounds, we were called to account for it. After some time on the repenting bench, we then discussed—in detail!—which of the laws we had broken and how we should have acted to live up to them.

For example, take the fight I had with my sister Brooke over the stolen toy. Brooke had a discussion about the importance of asking and respect, while I had to think about how I had broken the peace.

Looking back, I see that making the family laws just one word was a stroke of genius. Instead of coming up with an ever-changing list of specific rules, my dad expected us to internalize just five general ones. But those laws were carefully chosen to cover a wide range of possibilities, and there was deep intention behind each one. Let's dig a little deeper into what each law meant to my family:

Peace: Having a peaceful home was at the very top of my dad's list. To us, peace meant that the house was not loud and chaotic, but calm and quiet. The expectation was to maintain peace in your space, peace within yourself, and peace in your family. Many actions went along with the law of peace. For example, if you wanted to have a conversation with somebody, you went up to them, touched them on the shoulder, and waited until they were done with whatever they were doing and could speak with you. There was no shouting from room to room. There was a time for quiet and a time for being loud.

Asking: With four kids in the house, the concept of asking was huge, and it played a major role in providing boundaries for each of us growing up. We've seen how this law played out when it came to respecting personal property—you have to ask someone before you take their stuff! The law of asking also meant that we had to get permission from our parents to do things, whether it was sleeping over at a friend's house or going out for the night once we got to high school. The specific meaning of the law evolved as we got older and needed to ask for different things.

Order: While the law of peace is about people and how you interact with them, the law of order is about physical surroundings. My dad wanted a neat home, and he expected that we all pitched in to make it that way. In addition to cleaning our rooms every Saturday, my siblings and I were also each assigned a zone of the house that was our responsibility to straighten up, dust, and vacuum before we could move on to weekend fun. The law of order meant taking care of our things as well as shared spaces.

Respect: The law of respect has two parts: respecting yourself and respecting others. Self-respect means putting good healthy food into your body, exercising every day, keeping clean, and dressing nicely—my mom was adamant about wearing good clothes to church! Respecting others means being kind and courteous, not just to adults, but to siblings and peers. As I got older, I realized that respect also means being mindful of other cultures so you don't just assume you know what will make other people feel respected—you have to remain open to other people's perspectives on what respect looks like.

Obedience: Obedience and respect are closely related, and my parents felt it was important to spell out exactly how they wished to be respected. In our house, the law of obedience meant that we did as we were told, and we accepted the directions and answers we were given without an extended argument. A sassy attitude was very much against this law! This expectation also extended to teachers at school, and it was great training for working with future bosses. We learned from an early age that you did your job without complaining.

To make sure that we all understood the family laws, my dad added them to our out-loud-family-saying sessions before bed. After we went through the sayings, we also repeated the laws, so they were quickly memorized. Sometimes at the dinner table or before bed, my dad or mom would pick one law to discuss as a family. They would offer a platform, and we would each describe what peace or respect meant to us in that moment. These open-ended conversations allowed us to participate in creating a shared understanding and an environment of cooperation. They were also a great way to make sure that the meaning of the laws evolved as we grew up, since a six-year-old's focus will be very different from a sixteen-year-old's.

WHY FAMILY LAWS ARE IMPORTANT

Clearly stated family laws form the foundation for structure and routine in the home. The laws themselves encapsulate your expectations about your children's behavior and set the tone for the way your household operates. As you repeat and discuss the laws, you'll also be showing your children the outcomes you expect and putting in place consequences when the laws are broken.

In my family, the structure consisted of daily repetition of the laws, regular discussion about their meaning, and the repenting bench system of accountability when laws were broken. These routines formed the rhythm of our family life, and we always knew what to expect—and what was expected of us.

My dad grew up in a very strict household with solid routines like getting up at seven a.m. on a Saturday morning to wash the car or help out with household chores. For him, structure was natural. It's why so many of our family laws revolved around order and why the routines that grew out of those laws included a Saturday morning chore inspection that would put a military sergeant to shame. You don't have to model the same structures we had—in fact, I will probably not add obedience to my own list of family laws, and will try to offer plenty of choices when it comes to fulfilling family duties. But research does show that structure and routine are critical for child development.

It's clear to any new parent that babies need routines, including that all-important sleep schedule. As kids get older, routines are still important for providing a sense of safety and security. Psychologists report that a predictable structure to the day— homework, dinner, TV, bath, reading, and bedtime—helps children know what to expect and is a crucial part of helping them feel safe.[7] We've all seen a kid melt down into a tantrum when they're in a new place, up too late, or are dealing with a curveball that throws them off their game. Kids don't have a lot of control over what happens to them, and that can be very stressful. Providing structure and clarity is actually one of the kindest things a parent can do for a child. This is especially true these days, as anxiety diagnoses have skyrocketed for kids and teens—up 20 percent

---

[7] Robert Myers, "The Importance of a Regular Routine to Your Child," Child Development Institute, November 7, 2011, https://childdevelopmentinfo.com/family-building/the-importance-of-a-regular-routine-to-your-child/#gs.1v7258.

between 2007 and 2012,[8] long before a global pandemic made things even worse.

Knowing what to expect also helps kids gain confidence and begin to act independently. When you know you have to brush your teeth after a bath, you'll eventually grab that toothbrush and get the job done without a reminder! In addition to supporting healthy habits, predictable family structures support cognitive development and time management skills that will help your child succeed in school, work, and life in general.[9]

Structure and routine also play a role in creating healthy boundaries.[10] My parents always made us go to bed at eight o'clock, even in the summer. It was still light out, and we could hear the neighborhood kids running around outside, still having fun. Even if we complained or begged to stay up, the 8:00 p.m. lights-out was something we could always count on. The fact that my parents enforced this boundary made it clear to us that their rules were important. We knew that when they said something, they meant it.

---

[8] Amy Ellis Nutt "Why Kids and Teens May Face Far More Anxiety These Days," *The Washington Post*, May 10, 2018, https://www.washingtonpost.com/news/to-your-health/wp/2018/05/10/why-kids-and-teens-may-face-far-more-anxiety-these-days/.

[9] Amanda Stropes, "Back to School: Importance of Structure and Routine for Healthy Child Development," Families First, August 5, 2019, https://www.familiesfirstindiana.org/back-to-school-importance-of-structure-and-routine-for-healthy-child-development.

[10] "The Importance of Routine in Childhood," Melbourne Child Psychology and School Psychology Services, accessed May 27, 2021, https://www.melbournechildpsychology.com.au/blog/the-importance-of-routine-in-childhood/.

We may not have always liked the boundaries, but they ultimately helped us learn how to function within limits. My parents did a great job making home a place where we were taught to understand consequences, boundaries and rewards, and I benefited so much from having this solid foundation *before* I went out into the world. I didn't have to learn the hard way that a teacher or boss meant what they said. I already learned that at home, so I was ahead of the game.

That's what I want for my children, and I'm sure you want the same for yours: security, confidence, independence, and respect for boundaries. Family laws make it possible to provide a loving environment with predictable expectations and outcomes. And all it takes is a few carefully chosen words that your family will live by.

HOW TO DEVELOP YOUR
OWN FAMILY LAWS

When you're ready to dive into the work of creating your own family laws, it's important to remember that you and your partner come from very different backgrounds. Your goal is to be intentional in creating rules and values that you want to teach your children, but you'll also have to be intentional with each other first.

Even if you grew up in the same hometown, no two families are alike. You know very well what your own household was like and the expectations your parents had of you, but you'll need to work with your partner to combine two very different upbringings into one unified front. This can be challenging! I come from a household with a ton of structure, but my husband's family is much different. We've already had plenty of discussions about sharing chores and what we each want from our living space in these early months of marriage, and it's an ongoing conversation. The same is true for you and your partner as you explore making family laws together: it's a process.

To do this work, I encourage you both to consider the questions below. Once you've had a chance to think about your own childhood and your personal vision of what you want your family life to be like, it's time to come together to share your answers and find your common ground. You might agree on a lot, or you might have to have some deep discussions to figure out how to honor both of your views. This is really important work, so take your time on it.

Step One: Analyze the Household Structure You Grew Up With

Take some time to think back on what your own childhood was like. It's helpful to think about typical weekdays during the school year, since those are the most ordinary days—and the ones where you most likely experienced a set routine.

Answer these questions on your own first:

1. How would you describe the atmosphere and energy in your house when you were growing up? What were family interactions like?

2. What sort of systems and structures were in place? These could be specific rules as well as a general sense of how things worked.

3. What did you really like about your household structure as a child? Why?

4. What didn't you like about your parents' systems (or lack thereof)? Why?

5. What key takeaways from your childhood family systems would you like to continue for your children?

6. Is there anything from your own family experience that you want to avoid?

7. What are the most important things you would like to teach your children?

8. What do you want life inside your house to feel like on a daily basis? Why is this important to you?

Step Two: Come Together With Your Partner

Now that you have a clear vision of your own childhood, it's time to share your answers with your partner. But be sure to actively and openly listen to each answer—and try to set aside any preconceived ideas about how you assumed they would answer.

Then, discuss these questions together:

1. What do you agree on?

2. What do you disagree about?

3. Why do you disagree? (It might take some work to figure this out!)

Step Three: Choose Your Family Laws

I can still recite my own family's laws without even thinking about them because they were encapsulated in just one word. Those words let us know what was expected of us and transferred my parents' values directly to us in a completely accessible way.

What words might you use for your own family laws? I've provided a menu below to provide some inspiration. There's also space for you to add your own ideas.

Scan the list together with your partner, and work together to choose the words that most resonate with you. If you had many differences in your upbringing or some sticky disagreements about your vision for family structure, this exercise should help you focus on the values you have in common.

☐ asking	☐ obedience	☐ _____
☐ creativity	☐ order	☐ _____
☐ fun	☐ peace	☐ _____
☐ gratitude	☐ perseverance	☐ _____
☐ harmony	☐ reflection	☐ _____
☐ honesty	☐ resourcefulness	☐ _____
☐ integrity	☐ respect	☐ _____
☐ kindness	☐ responsibility	☐ _____

If you're having trouble deciding, don't stress about it! The point isn't to find the perfect word, but just to zero in on the idea behind it. Just pick something close for now—you can always update and change it as your family grows and changes.

Step Four: Develop the Ideas Behind the Words

Once you've selected a few words that really speak to you for your family laws, it's time to think in depth about the meaning behind them. What does each word mean to you and your family?

You could discuss this with your partner just like we used to do around the dinner table, giving each other a chance to say what the word means to you in a few sentences. But I'd like to suggest a more visionary question for you to explore:

What will our family life look like when we achieve _____

_____?

Fill in the blank with one of the words you've chosen. Then answer this question collaboratively with your partner to paint a picture of the type of life you want to live with your children. As you each add to the vision, you'll be coming up with expectations for how you interact with each other. These will develop into the actions suggested by the one-word law. As you flesh out this picture of your family's future together, you'll also tap into your feelings about the law and why it's so important to you.

For example, let's say you chose "creativity" as one of your family laws. What will it look like when your family achieves creativity? You may decide that it means weekends built around arts and crafts. Your partner may add a desire for creative problem solving instead of complaining. You may both ban the concept of boredom from your house or decide to limit screen time in favor of creative activities.

This is a powerful exercise that will bring clarity to your vision for family life. It's worth completing for each word you've chosen to turn into law, but remember that this is just the beginning. You don't have to come up with every possible contingency related to the law right now. Family laws will evolve naturally over time.

In this chapter, we learned how to create family laws to structure your household routines and expectations. Because family laws are just one word each, even small children can memorize them quickly and engage in discussions about their importance. Making family laws broad also gives parents an easy way to correct misbehavior that doesn't involve negotiations over an ever-growing list of specific rules. The conversations you have around family laws will change over time as your children grow.

Providing clear expectations and boundaries for your children is critical to their overall development. When children know what to expect from family rules and routines, they feel safe and secure, and they learn to act independently within the structures you've created. This foundation leads to the development of healthy habits, respect for authority, and self-reliance that will help them be successful in adulthood.

You have the power to be very intentional about the way your household runs, so don't leave it to chance. If you're not intentional about creating structures for your children, the *lack* of routine and rules will then become the norm. Negative norms are just as powerful as positive ones. They will leave your children feeling unsettled and uncertain of their place within your family and the world at large. When you establish family laws, you get everyone on the same page, working together to create the type of family you've always wanted.

Creating clear, accessible family laws provides a solid foundation for everything that comes after—including lessons about financial responsibility. But life isn't all rules, rules, rules, and I didn't spend every waking moment on the repenting bench or taking care of household chores. We also had lots of fun together—and your family should, too.

3

MAKE
TRADITIONS FUN

Our family law of order led to a very structured Saturday routine. There was no sleeping in for the Cornetet kids! We woke up early, had breakfast, and then my dad would send us off to clean our room and our zone. I had the living room, so it was my job to dust the shelves and tabletops, vacuum the floors, and make sure the throw pillows were all nicely arranged on the sofa. I also had to put away anything that wasn't in its place.

While I worked on that, Brooke cleaned the bathrooms, Claire did the dining room, and my brother Peter made sure the kitchen was in good order after breakfast. We all cleaned our rooms, too, so beds were made and clothes were picked up with lightning speed.

We worked quickly because we knew what was coming next: Dad would call us all back to the living room and have us stand at attention in front of him. Then he would march us to our zones and our rooms for an inspection to make sure they were cleaned well.

Did I mention my dad would have made a great army general?

We knew when our work was approved because he would say, "Okay, go grab your notebooks."

It was time for Dad's Class.

For the next twenty minutes, we sat around a table and got Dad's full attention as he taught us a specific lesson about saving, spending, compound interest, the importance of a strong handshake—anything he had decided was important for us to know in life.

And when we put our pencils down, it was time to brainstorm what we would do together for the rest of the day. This was a reward for hard work well done, and it was also the way my parents made sure we spent quality time together.

Sometimes we went to the movies, or maybe we had a picnic or took a bike ride. We always did something fun, but my favorite Saturdays were the ones spent at Barnes & Noble, the giant bookstore in town. I remember Dad calling out that the bus was leaving, so all six of us climbed into the Suburban and headed off for an hour of browsing.

I immediately headed for the shelf of mysteries to pick out the next few Nancy Drew books. Brooke made a beeline to the fantasy section, while my parents roamed the whole store. There was something almost magical about the hush of the bookstore and the faint aroma of the coffee shop in the back, and online shopping just doesn't compare. To this day I love the serendipity of picking a book and leafing through it without knowing what to expect. Will you find something amazing as you flip through its pages? We were allowed to choose anything that caught our attention, and in this way, I learned about everything from the national park system to the nighttime sky.

My dad loved to read and wanted to pass that on to us, so we were allowed to pick out a few books to buy on these Saturdays. When we got home, we'd spend a quiet afternoon reading, each of us curled up in a favorite cozy spot and enjoying the quiet companionship of the day. The books would give us plenty of fuel for the next week's dinnertime conversation. The simple Saturday afternoon at the bookstore was one of my favorite family traditions because I could explore the world and enjoy being surrounded by my family as well. It was perfect for me.

ADDING FUN
TO FAMILY ROUTINES

In the previous chapter, we explored the importance of structure and routine for children. But those routines aren't always about following the rules and facing consequences. It's equally important to be intentional about having fun as a family, which will help you establish close relationships with each other.

Fun comes in so many forms. It can be quiet, like our Saturday bookstore trips and afternoon reading sessions. It can be loud, like a family karaoke and dance party. It can be playing silly games while you clean, or it can be about getting dirty on summer camping trips. Fun will look different for everyone, but the point is to spend quality time together on a regular basis.

Like every family, we had our special holiday traditions that came up once a year. But my parents knew that leaving quality time to chance in the weeks and months between holidays would leave too much room for things to slip through the cracks. So instead of focusing only on big traditions, my parents were intentional about creating daily, weekly, and monthly traditions that created predictable structure and made room for love and laughter each day.

Daily routines included lots of the basics of habit-building, like cleaning up our rooms, brushing our teeth, and picking out our clothes for the next day. These things weren't necessarily fun on their own, but my parents did a good job finding ways to make boring, repetitive tasks fun. For example, when we brushed our teeth, we would sing "Twinkle, Twinkle Little Star" to keep track of the time. When the song was done, we knew we had brushed long enough. My mom often added music to our day and used songs to help us learn things like the fifty states. And, of course, our out-loud family sayings were designed to be fun by keeping us active and providing opportunities to connect with our parents through conversation.

On a weekly basis, my dad made sure that weekends were filled with quality family time. This included our cleaning routine on Saturdays and the fun of marching from room to room together. When we sat down for Dad's Class, he created lessons that were fun for us. There was always a hands-on component that brought ideas about business and finance to life in a way we could understand. We also had a weekly dance party together around our state-of-the-art (for the early 1990s) player piano. This modern wonder had a slot for floppy disks full of songs that the piano would then play on its own—perfect for my family of music lovers who couldn't play any instruments. That was a blast for all of us and a great way to get out our kid energy in a safe, constructive way.

Once a month, we had parent dates. This was a special afternoon you would spend with either Mom or Dad, and they let us pick whatever activity we wanted: lunch at a favorite restaurant, a picnic in the park, horseback riding—as long as it was something fun to do together, anything was on the table. Most parent dates were pretty simple, and my favorites were just going out to lunch and having time to talk. With four children, my parents knew things could get chaotic, so they committed to making sure we each had individual attention. That one-on-one time nurtured close connections and made each of us feel special.

WHY FUN FAMILY TRADITIONS ARE IMPORTANT

On a very practical level, my dad used fun as a way to reward us for good behavior. We had a little chart on the fridge that we would use to check off all of our daily chores and responsibilities, and sometimes we'd get a surprise trip to the ice cream stand as a reward for getting everything done. I vividly remember piling into the car as the sun was setting and driving off to get a treat. My dad had a very clear vision of what he wanted us to learn and how he wanted our household to feel, but he also knew that if it wasn't fun, we wouldn't ever want to do any of those things. In that respect, fun traditions went hand-in-hand with the family law of peace, as it provided balance and ensured buy-in from the kids— instead of setting up conflict over rules and expectations. Mary Poppins wasn't wrong about that spoonful of sugar! If you want your kids to embrace your family laws and routines, rewarding the behavior you want to see is key.

My dad also achieved buy-in by getting all the kids involved in family decision-making. He knew that if he gave us choices, we would have more ownership of the activities we did together as a family. On the Saturdays that we didn't go to the bookstore, Dad would lead a planning session to decide how we would spend the weekend. He would choose one of us to be the scribe and write down everyone's ideas during our big brainstorming session. Dad made sure everyone was included, so if Claire hadn't offered an idea, he would make sure to call on her so everyone was represented. After looking over all the ideas, Dad would narrow it down to the top two choices, and we would vote on how we wanted to spend our family time. By giving us a say, we all knew our opinions mattered, and we had a stronger interest in and connection to our family time.

This simple act of making sure everyone is heard is something experts recommend for building strong family bonds. In a fact sheet with advice about building family relationships, the University of Delaware recommends active listening, giving everyone a chance to share their thoughts, and spending time together[11]—something our weekly quality-time planning sessions covered quite nicely. Including your children in the decision-making process gives them a sense of ownership and helps build confidence in their position as a valuable, respected member of

----

[11] University of Delaware Cooperative Extension, "Building Strong Family Relationships." University of Delaware, accessed May 31, 2021, https://www.udel.edu/canr/cooperative-extension/fact-sheets/building-strong-family-relationships/.

your family unit. That very basic sense of being valued is the foundation of strong self-esteem that your kids will carry with them as they move out into the world.

This sense of acceptance and belonging takes time to develop, but having strong routines and rituals that reinforce family bonds ensure that the message of love comes across daily, weekly, and monthly—no matter what else might be going on in the world. In my family, this meant that four very different siblings all still felt accepted, even though in many ways we were nothing alike. Our rituals silently but clearly said, "We love you. We accept you. You always have a safe place here. You can always come home."

In a major review of the past fifty years of research on family rituals and routines, researchers from Syracuse University found that strong family traditions are "regulators of development" that help children grow into competent adults. They also suggest that routines and rituals may "ease the stress of daily living" for even very busy families.[12] And just in case you're a parent in one of those very busy families, the researchers also pointed out that there's no right or wrong way to create family rituals: success depends on choosing things that feel natural, and there's plenty of room for variation to reflect your culture and values.

---

[12] Barbara H. Fiese et al, "A Review of 50 Years of Research on Naturally Occurring Family Routines and Rituals: Cause for Celebration?" *Journal of Family Psychology*, 2002, https://www.apa.org/pubs/journals/releases/fam-164381.pdf.

Finally, the fun you have as a family gives you the opportunity to create shared memories. Whether your kids remember your nightly bedtime routine or your monthly trip to the candy store, shared memories will bond your kids to each other and to you as parents. It's a gift that keeps on giving, as the memories of fun times can be recalled again and again, long after your children have grown up. These shared memories bind you together across generations, no matter what you do together: going to the beach, playing pickleball, or sharing a bedtime story.

As a kid, I was definitely focused on the fun for its own sake. Can we go to the bookstore? How about the movies? When's the next shopping trip with Mom? But now that I'm an adult, I see clearly that my dad's love language was quality time. It was really important for him as a father to be not just around but *paying attention*. All of the family rituals and traditions my parents put in place created opportunities to check in with us. How were we doing? What was challenging us, and what were we looking forward to? In particular, parent dates allowed the time and space for us simply to talk, and it gave our parents insight into who we were at any given moment. That's especially important for busy families, since it's so easy to focus on jumping from task to task instead of clearly seeing the unique individual standing in front of you.

Life moves fast and childhood is short. If you don't intentionally carve out time to enjoy it while it's happening, you might wake up one day to find that you missed it.

HOW TO DEVELOP YOUR OWN
FAMILY TRADITIONS

I could go on and on about my own family traditions, but you don't need to emulate what I grew up with. Your family is completely different, because you and your partner come to the table with your own ideas and values—and that doesn't even take into account the personalities of your children!

The big question to consider is: What is it that you do that makes your traditions fun? In my house growing up, daily family dinner was super important. But if your family has a crazy schedule that makes a sit-down dinner impossible, what do you do instead? Do you have a totally different daily routine that you can make more fun, or do you find a way to make dinner on the go special too?

There's no right way to run your daily, weekly and monthly routines —but you do have to be intentional about planning them.

Step One: Analyze What You Already Do

Take a moment to think about your family life as it is right now. You probably already do a bunch of things together that you enjoy, so start there. Once you start thinking about your daily, weekly, and monthly routines, you'll be able to pick out things that are already fun.

And if you get stuck while trying to think of fun things to do together, don't worry! It happens, and it's perfectly normal— especially after a pandemic that forced us to change our routines. I encourage you to think about even the smallest things you do for fun, from spending a moment to find the moon each night to singing a song while washing your hands. There is no such thing as too small when it comes to having fun with your kids. They will delight in all of it.

Brainstorm your answers below.

What do you already do with your family that you enjoy?

- Daily activities:

- Weekly activities:

- Monthly activities:

- Yearly activities / special occasions:

Now take a look back over your answers. Do you notice a pattern about the types of activities you enjoy? Maybe it's that all your favorite activities together are outdoors, or maybe you enjoy creative projects. As you already know, my parents valued some quiet time, so they found a way to get it with our Saturday reading time after those trips to the bookstore.

As you look over the things you already do together, think about how you can build on that foundation. Can you take these things a step further? Explore ways this might work by answering these questions:

1. What are some of the themes you see in the activities you enjoy together?

2. How can you build off of those themes to add more fun to your routines? Brainstorm a bit.

3. How can you be more intentional about making sure that something you all enjoy together happens every day?

4. What might you stop doing to give more space and time for more activities together?

Remember, by building on what you already have in place, you don't have to build any new habits. Just carve out time to devote to the things you love in a more intentional way. You can even ask your kids for their ideas about this—their creativity might surprise you!

Step Two: Explore Your Aspirations

Remember when you spent time spelling out what you wanted your household and family life to feel like back in Chapter 2? That work is the basis for everything else. When you're intentional about building a family life around your values, everything that you do with your children—from breakfast routines to the way you spend your Saturday nights—is an opportunity to instill the values and lessons you want them to learn.

So go ahead and review your work in Chapter 2 now.

Once you've done that, think about how you can add fun traditions and routines that support your vision for your family. In my family, my dad decided he wanted to spend more time with us, but that he also wanted to do more educational activities. That led him to question how he could best use our weekends together. His flash of inspiration was to make the family outing educational by taking us to the bookstore. That's how he was able to take the general goal of quality time and tweak it to support his value of making our time together educational.

Of course, my parents also just loved to buy books. You don't have to go to the bookstore if you prefer the library—and you don't have to sit around and read on a Saturday if your idea of fun is hiking, surfing, or singing in a choir.

The trick is to decide what's meaningful to you and get creative about adding those values to your routines.

Answer the questions below to deepen your thinking about your values.

1. What do you want to be doing with your family but aren't doing yet?

2. If you could design the perfect family day, what would it look like?

3. Refer back to your family values. List your five big words here.

4. For each value, list activities, routines and traditions that you already do that support these. It's okay if some have a lot of support and others are blank!

5. How can you get creative about adding additional traditions that support more of your values? Take some time to brainstorm new ideas for each value.

6. Review those same responses to the five questions in this section: which feel the most doable to you? Why?

7. Review those same responses to the five questions in this section: which feel the most challenging to accomplish? Why?

Step Three: Commit to Daily, Weekly,
and Monthly Fun

It takes time to build any new habit—even fun ones. It's best to start small, with just one to three new activities in the beginning. As you build them into your routines and they become second nature, you'll be able to add even more fun to your agenda.

Look back over your answers to the questions in the previous section. What activities stand out as the most fun and/or easiest to accomplish? Choose three activities to add to this chart:

Daily Fun	Weekly Fun	Monthly Fun

If you're having trouble choosing, don't sweat it. Just pick one activity that sounds like fun and go with it. You can always try it for a few weeks or months, and if it doesn't work out, you can cross it out and replace it with something new. For example, if your kids were really into flying kites in the spring but they got tired of it by September, nobody wants you to go on forced kite-flying expeditions! Keep an open mind and an open dialogue so that family fun is just that: actually fun for everyone. Family traditions will grow and change with your family, and that's exactly as it should be.

One of the best ways to make sure you stick to your new commitment is to hold yourself accountable. I recommend scanning and printing out this chart, or making a poster of it, so you can put it where everyone can see it. Your kids will definitely not let you forget Sunday pancakes or that monthly trip to the water slides!

Remember, you can add routines to the chart at any time too. Fun has a way of multiplying itself, so you're sure to think of more activities to add. Once you get the first new routines under your belt, the sky's the limit when it comes to adding more fun to your family life.

KEY TAKEAWAYS

Create Daily, Weekly, & Monthly Activities

Define Fun for Your Family

Include Kids in Planning

In this chapter, we learned how to carve out time for family fun. In addition to the big touchstone events like vacations and holiday celebrations, it's important to create daily, weekly, and monthly routines that thoughtfully add fun to your family life. Every family has a different definition of fun, and you can begin the process by taking stock of what you already enjoy and finding ways to build these things into the rhythms of your life together.

Providing opportunities for fun helps your children build shared memories that strengthen family bonds. When you include kids in the decision-making process, you show them that their opinions are valued, which helps build self-esteem and confidence. Spending time with your children individually allows the space for deeper connections that will help you understand and guide them through difficulties. Life isn't always fun, but making sure you strike a balance between work and play will ensure that your relationship is strong enough to weather any challenge.

In my life, my family bonds were never more clear than they were when my parents and siblings made the trek to my home for my son's funeral. It was in the middle of the pandemic, but they were there for me, and it *mattered*. That bond is deeply rooted in all the time we spent together growing up—there's just no substitute for that. By intentionally choosing to make family time a priority when we were little, my parents created the support system I would rely on for my whole life.

Now that I'm the adult, I find myself making dates with my husband and friends so that we can spend quality time together. Sure, my husband and I had *plenty* of alone time during the pandemic, but as life gets back to normal, weekly dates will be key in staying connected. I also have yoga dates with friends and regular trips with my siblings, all of which give me the time to nurture those relationships. It's easy to get busy and let friendships slip away, but my dad's Saturday planning sessions taught me how important it is to schedule time for fun and connection with the people you love.

But how do you pay for all that fun? Your kids will need to understand the basics of money to keep the good times rolling as they become adults.

4

ESTABLISH A FAMILY ECONOMY

One morning, when I was about seven years old, my dad sat me down at the kitchen table. "I have something for you," he said. I sat in my chair, swinging my legs back and forth since they couldn't yet reach the floor.

He placed a jelly bean on the table in front of me. "You can have this jelly bean right now if you want. I have to do something in the other room. But if you wait to eat it until I come back, I'll give you another jelly bean."

I don't remember which option I went for that day. What I do remember is the choice. It blew my little kid's mind: Eat it up now or get an extra one? What should I do?

Fast forward to the same kitchen table, with me in the same chair. This time my feet did reach the floor, because I was about ten. My dad reached into his pocket and pulled out a handful of gold coins. He placed them on the table in front of me. They were those Sacagawea gold dollars, and they were so shiny. They must have been brand new. I had never seen anything like them.

"Each of these coins is worth one dollar. You have ten, so you have ten dollars. We're going shopping this afternoon, and they're yours to spend any way you want. But if you can wait until next Saturday without spending any of them, I will double it with another stack of coins."

This time, I remember exactly what I did: I went shopping but didn't buy a single thing. I wanted more of those beautiful coins, and I was willing to wait. And sure enough, Dad presented me with ten more Sacagawea coins the following week.

I was hooked. I just got a whole lot of gold coins, and that was super cool. I felt like a rock star.

This, of course, was my dad's version of the famous Stanford marshmallow test.[13] In case you missed its resurgence on social media, this is the one in which researchers offered young children one marshmallow now or two if they could wait to eat it. Back in the 1970s, the researchers concluded that the ability to delay gratification was strongly correlated to better life outcomes overall. While the original results are now generally taken with a grain of salt, my dad was intrigued by their implication, and he was determined to make sure we understood—and could eventually exercise—delayed gratification.

THE FOUNDATIONS
OF OUR FAMILY ECONOMY

Looking back on it as an adult, I understand that this lesson in delayed gratification laid the foundation for our whole family economy. It was our first introduction to *value* and forced us to wrestle with this question:

Which is worth more to you: the pleasure the money brings right now, or the certainty of having more money later?

By swapping out candy for gold coins, my dad placed this learning squarely into the context of financial lessons. The coins turned

---

[13] B.J. Casey et al, "Behavioral and Neural Correlates of Delay of Gratification 40 Years Later," Proceedings of the National Academy of Sciences of the United States, Vol. 108, No. 36. September 6, 2011, 14998–15003, https://www.pnas.org/content/108/36/14998.full.

the more general joy of the jelly bean into a concrete lesson about money. We got to use those coins as real money on shopping trips and later as deposits in the Cornetet Family Bank (which we'll talk more about in the next chapter). The lesson was so tangible, and we learned by doing: whether we spent or saved, we felt those coins in our hands. We knew what they were worth because we could do the math to see how many books or bags of candy we could buy.

We also learned to assess value on our own terms. My sister Brooke loved sugar, so she would happily spend her coins at the candy store to enjoy a sweet moment. In my case, I really liked the coins and the way I felt knowing I always had a bunch of them. My dad never tried to tell us what to buy, and he never told us not to spend our money. We always had the choice, and that freedom to explore and experiment with real money helped us figure out what it meant to us.

What will the money achieve for you? That's its real value.

Understanding the value of money meant that we were ready for the fundamentals of a family economy, which my dad—as usual!—summed up succinctly: earn, save, spend.

These three words were added to our poster of out-loud family sayings and family laws. They were the core of what my dad wanted to teach us about money: you had to earn it; next, you paid yourself by saving it; and *then* you could spend whatever you had left. The order was important, and our family economy was set up to make sure we learned it.

LESSONS IN EARNING, SAVING AND SPENDING

Although Dad freely gave us the Sacagawea coins as part of the lesson on delayed gratification, he made it very clear that money was something you had to *earn*. Even when we were very little, he talked about the work he was doing. He definitely wasn't a parent who mysteriously disappeared during the day or kept his work life separate from his family. Since he worked from home, we got to watch him in action, and he spent a lot of time explaining what he did and connecting the dots that this is how our family had money for our house, clothes, and food. Money was *always* a part of everyday conversation.

Dad also made sure that our understanding of earning was very concrete. Talking about the value of work is one thing, but actually having to do it is another! Cleaning our rooms and zones was part of our duty to the family and was therefore unpaid, but Dad created a list of extra chores that we could do to earn more money. He posted the jobs and their wages right next to the poster of family sayings and laws, and we could choose whatever we wanted—or not to do any of them at all.

Just as the choice to spend or save our gold coins helped us understand the value of money, the choice of jobs helped us understand the value of our time. On a hot day, washing the car for ten dollars was a lot more fun than cleaning out a stifling garage. We learned to choose the jobs we liked best, were good at, or could do well to maximize our time and make the earning more enjoyable—valuable skills for the future, when we would have to decide on our adult careers.

I was about eight years old when my parents first posted the chore list, and the jobs became more strenuous and complex as we grew. We were also encouraged to be creative about finding work outside of the home. By the time I was twelve, I babysat all over the neighborhood, making good money in a way that I found *much* easier than organizing the basement. Brooke figured out that she could get up early and collect cans and bottles for the deposit money, while my brother Peter eventually tried his hand at every odd job under the sun, including selling pumpkins on my uncle's farm and working at a Honey Baked Ham shop. My sister Claire was very artistic so by the time she was in high school she made and sold hand-decorated sweatshirts to all her friends.

Whether we worked for an employer, for family, or cobbled something together for ourselves, we were always encouraged to work and earn. Even though my parents highly valued education, they did not buy into the notion that school was our job. On the contrary, they firmly believed that work experiences were a crucial part of our education.

Working and learning at the same time has a long tradition in my family. My grandfather paid his own way at Michigan State by working forty hours per week and attending class all the while. With that example in our ancestry, there were no excuses for not being able to get decent grades and hold a part-time job at the same time! Earning was an essential part of learning, not a distraction from it.

Once our family economy provided ways for us to earn money on our own, it was time to learn about saving it. We'll talk more about the specific mechanism for making lessons in savings concrete in the next chapter. My dad also taught us directly about compound interest to reinforce the importance of delayed gratification and the power of saving over time.

Specifically, my dad hammered home the Rule of 72 in his Saturday classes. I still have a notebook filled with math problems using the Rule of 72 to figure out how long it would take to double my savings at a given interest rate. The Rule of 72 is an easy way to understand the power of compound interest, and it's doable for kids as soon as they learn division in math class.

Here's how the Rule of 72 works:

72 ÷ interest rate = years to double your money

Let's say you have $100,000 in savings, and you invest it in an account with a 5 percent interest rate. 72 ÷ 5 = 14 (give or take a few months), so in fourteen years you will have $200,000. In another fourteen years you will have $400,000. How long will it take you to become a millionaire?

My dad loved that question. He also liked to use really big interest rates to get us excited about the possibilities. We were always allowed to spend our money, but he would regularly quiz on compound interest scenarios using the Rule of 72 to reinforce the power of saving and investing. Doing the math ourselves helped us internalize the concept, and to this day, I still find myself calculating when my investments will double.

If you're having trouble keeping track of all the math, that's okay! Here's a chart to help you visualize the Rule of 72 and understand why investing early makes all the difference when it comes to harnessing the power of compound interest:

Compound Interest
RULE OF 72

Here are some interest rates to compare—as you can see, modest increases in rates have a dramatic effect on the doubling time

Years	1.5%	3%	6%	12%
0	$10,000	$10,000	$10,000	$10,000
6				$20,000
12	*In times of historically low interest rates, it's especially important to start investing early*		$20,000	$40,000
18				$80,000
24		$20,000	$40,000	$160,000
30				$320,000
36			$80,000	$640,000
42				$1,280,000
48	$20,000	$40,000	$160,000	$2,560,000

Though we were very much encouraged to earn and save, we also had to learn about spending and how to do it responsibly. We talked all the time about things we were thinking of buying, how much they cost, and whether they were worth the money (and, by extension, the time it took to earn that money). My parents did this everywhere, from the grocery store to a gift shop on vacation, so they modeled the type of deep thinking about money they wanted us to adopt.

We were also given plenty of hands-on practice in budgeting for our needs. For example, in high school my mom gave each of us a $200 budget for clothes shopping. We wore uniforms to school, but we were allowed to choose whatever we wanted for the rest of our wardrobe. This was a huge lesson in value and planning. So did Brooke *really* want that $100 pair of jeans from Limited Too? (She did.) Did those jeans make her feel confident and empowered? Or was it better to spread the money out over less expensive items so you could have more variety? Would they last through the year if they were too cheap? We learned those lessons by doing. If we made a mistake, we had to live with it—or use some of our own money to fix it.

By creating opportunities for us to earn, save, and spend, my parents built a miniature family economy that let us learn by doing. Our family economy provided years of hands-on learning that there's just no substitute for, and we were way ahead of the financial game when we set out on our own.

WHY YOU NEED TO TALK
TO YOUR KIDS ABOUT MONEY

We all knew that money was important from the moment my dad added "Earn, Save, Spend" to our poster of out-loud family sayings. My parents made a conscious choice to instill values in us from a very early age because they wanted to steer the conversation. You could say that my dad's deep desire for order just led him to add one more thing to the list of sayings and chores, but in truth, it's so much more than that.

Because here's the thing: If you aren't intentional about talking to your kids about money—if you don't make the choice to have those conversations—they're still going to learn about your money attitudes. In fact, researchers in the United Kingdom and Norway found that parent behavior has a direct influence on the way their children grow up to respond to economic problems and decision making.[14]

Money is a hugely emotional topic.[15] Like it or not, we all have an emotional response to money and what it can do for us, what it means to have it, what it feels like to lack it, how we worry about it or worship it or work for it.

Many people avoid talking to their children about money because they have a deep fear around the topic. They may want to protect their children from their anxieties, or they just want to avoid getting emotional in front of their children. It can be challenging for parents because they haven't worked through their own

[14] Paul Webley and Ellen K. Nyhus, "Parents' Influence On Children's Future Orientation and Saving," *Journal of Economic Psychology*, 2006. 140–164, https://home.uia.no/ellenkn/WebleyNyhus2006.pdf.

[15] Deevra Norling, "Money Is Not About Finances, It's About Emotion," *The Huffington Post*, June 16, 2015, https://www.huffpost.com/entry/money-is-not-about-financ_b_7579746.

unresolved emotions to talk about issues with their kids. (And there's nothing like becoming a parent to shine a light on anything left unresolved from your own childhood!)

There's also a lot of judgment wrapped up in our finances. Maybe you constantly worry that you don't have enough, or you struggled as a child with the sense that you didn't fit in because your family didn't have the same luxuries that others did. That fear of rejection or of worrying that you don't really belong in your place in society can create feelings that last for decades.

The point here isn't that you have to completely resolve all of your own feelings about money to be an effective parent. If that were true, we'd all fall short! But you do want to be mindful about your feelings as they arise so that you can discuss them openly with your children in an age-appropriate way.

Let me give an example of why open discussion is so important. In my family, my grandmother always said, "It's better to be a lady of the evening than to touch your principal." This was a lesson she had learned from her father, and she passed it down to my aunt and my dad, and eventually to me and my siblings.

But let's pick that apart for a minute. The idea here is that my great-grandfather believed it would literally be better for my grandmother to *resort to prostitution* than to dip into the principal of her investments if she was ever short on money. That's intense!

That story stuck with her, and she retold it often. Though it was mostly delivered with humor, the lesson that was passed down was emotional—it tapped into a deep and gendered fear about what it meant to be a "lady". Prostitution represented a total moral failure that would place any woman well outside of accepted norms. She'd be ostracized. And yet those consequences were all preferable to tapping into her principal, which was presented as an even more devastating moral failure.

That lesson as it was taught and learned through the generations can also make it hard to make decisions about money without a lot of angst, particularly if you're a woman who heard the warning loud and clear about how to be a "good girl." In general, it's great advice not to dip into your investments if you can help it, but there are definitely exceptions to the rule.

So what happens when it's time to consider dipping into the principal? It becomes an internal struggle to apply logic and good sense against that very powerful voice from childhood telling you never to touch the investment. This could inadvertently lead to making suboptimal decisions about the money—or at the very least, cause a good deal of anxiety wrestling with the pros and cons.

But what would it look like to open a discussion about money that faced the emotions around this issue head-on? A good start would be to acknowledge how crazy it is to encourage prostitution as an alternative to selling off an investment—and how did that make my grandmother feel? In what ways did she act on that advice, and how did she feel when she did? Sharing those thoughts with her own children and grandchildren would be powerful, and could go a long way toward stepping out of the long shadow cast by that family saying.

Next, imagine opening the conversation to include dialogue about what money—and investments—are for. Is its greatest purpose to provide security? Fun and adventure? Charitable help to others? These are value questions, and your answers may be different from mine. And they may be different from your own children's. By laying the foundation for an open, ongoing discussion about those values, you will provide your children the tools they need to develop their own ideas about the importance of money in their lives—no fear required.

HOW YOU CAN START YOUR OWN FAMILY ECONOMY

The whole point of developing a family economy is that you want to give your children a laboratory where they can practice some hands-on learning with money. When paired with rich, open conversations about your personal philosophy, feelings, and experiences around money, your hands-on family economy will lay the foundation for your children's economic education.

Specifically, they'll need opportunities to practice how to earn, save, and spend money. You can provide these in your family when children are as young as seven or eight—no need to wait until they're old enough to open their own checking account!

If building a family money system from scratch feels overwhelming, relax. You don't have to build a replica of the entire US economy for your kids! You can and should implement it gradually.

To help you get started on this project, consider your answers to the following questions.

1. What activities do you already do with your kids around earning, saving, and spending that you can build on? (allowances, paid odd jobs, a passbook savings account, grandparents savings bonds, trips to the mall, etc.)

Earning Activity	Saving Activity	Spending Activity

2. To give your family economy some structure, think about how often you talk about or do each of the activities you listed in question 1. Organize them into this chart:

Daily Activity	Weekly Activity	Monthly Activity

3. Take a moment to reflect on your existing family economy in the charts you filled out. (Remember, you're teaching your kids about money all the time, whether you're intentional about it or not!) In what areas are you doing well?

4. What areas would you like to improve upon—and why?

If you're uncertain how to build up your family economy in certain areas, check out some of these ideas for inspiration:

For Earning

- Establish a weekly allowance based on age.

- Create a list of chores or odd jobs and the rates you'll pay your kids to do them.

- Become an angel investor by giving your kids some initial funds to start a small business.

- Help your kids brainstorm age-appropriate jobs based on their interests.

- Hold a family yard sale and let your kids keep the money their items bring in.

For Saving

- Start a savings jar to provide a visual as the money increases.

- Come up with family savings goals that you all contribute to—perhaps for a weekend outing or a meal at your favorite restaurant.

- Consider setting up a system for parental matching funds to encourage your kids to save.

For Spending

- Talk about the cost of everyday items (groceries, clothing, movie tickets, etc.).

- Invite your kids to family budget meetings.

- Give your kids a budget for snacks, clothing, or weekend activities and let them make their own spending decisions.

- Start your own family bank. (See Chapter 5 for details!)

KEY TAKEAWAYS

Earn, Save, Spend

What Do You Already Do?

Start Your Family Economy

In this chapter, we learned how to create a family economy that gives children the opportunity to practice financial skills in a hands-on way from an early age. Focusing on the basics of earning, saving and spending—in that order!—will help your kids learn the value of a dollar and reinforce your family values as you model and discuss financial behaviors.

Starting early is key, as research has shown that parents have an enormous influence on their children's financial education. In particular, helping children develop tolerance for delayed gratification and an appreciation of the power of saving over the long term can set them up for financial success in the future. Providing practical opportunities to experience earning, saving, and spending through structured activities and regular conversation will help maintain an open dialogue—one that you can intentionally steer rather than just hoping for the best.

In that moment at the kitchen table when I realized I could double my gold coins if I just didn't spend them, I became a saver. From then on, whether I was working for other people or running my own business, I always took advantage of whatever type of savings plan was offered to me. I loved being able to make my 401(k) savings automatic and being able to watch it grow, just as the Rule of 72 showed me it would. Even in my early twenties, I never hesitated to pay myself first, and today my retirement savings are solid.

My 401(k) wasn't my first experience in investing, though. That came years earlier and was another part of our Saturday family routine: the Cornetet National Bank.

5

THE CORNETET
NATIONAL BANK

When I was about eight, one of my favorite places to go was this gift shop near our house. It was a little place in a strip mall, nestled between a bike shop and a cafe. Inside, there were these huge displays of so many amazing things. I'm sure it's all bigger in my memory than it was in real life, but I could spend hours there browsing the shelves.

My favorite area was the display of animal figurines. There were Disney dalmatians and all sorts of little statuettes, many of which would mark a special birthday or milestone. They were definitely designed to be collected. One section of the display was a woodland scene filled with tiny forest animals.

Among the foxes and bears and bunnies, one animal stood out: the wolf.

This little figurine was *adorable*. It was made of wood and hand-painted in the rich colors of the forest. And it had these big round eyes that looked right up at me in perfect cuteness.

I wanted it.

I picked it up and checked the bottom for the price tag: twenty dollars.

That was a big purchase, since my allowance at the time was just eight dollars a week—one dollar per year of our age. But bigger than the price was the emotional weight of the purchase. At that age, I was pretty stingy with my money, and I never felt like anything I could buy felt as good as watching my allowance savings add up each week. I very much liked to add, not subtract.

I stood there for what felt like hours, trying to decide if I should buy it or not. Was it worth it? I know I didn't buy it the first time I saw it, but I went back to the store every few weeks and tried to figure out if I really wanted it.

I bought it. And oh my gosh, my eight-year-old heart was happy with that purchase. The rush of handing the clerk my own money, watching her carefully wrap the wolf in tissue and place it in the bag felt good.

That feeling lasted for about a week. Then, the following Saturday, it was time to settle my account at the Cornetet National Bank with my dad. I was a lot less excited to write down the word "minus" in my ledger, and it stung that I had to subtract such a big amount. In my head I was already doing the math to see how long it would take me to pay myself back with my allowance or how many extra chores I would have to do to get back to where I was.

Still, I was happy to have the wolf. My first big purchase taught me a lot of things about how to decide if something is valuable. Was it worth it to spend the money once the instant gratification and the buyer's high wore off? I'm still asking myself these questions today about everything from what we spend on rent and vacations to whether a creative Halloween costume is worth the effort. (It almost always is!)

THE FAMILY BANK AS
A LEARNING LABORATORY

In the previous chapter, we discussed the importance of earning, saving, and spending as the three fundamental economic activities to teach your children. These are the lessons of a lifetime, and no one gets to skip or ignore them. (Unless, of course, you win the Game of Life and never have to work for a living!)

For most of us, however, these are the rules: Everybody has to earn. Everybody has to save. Everybody has to spend—and get their spending habits under control to develop a good relationship with money.

To tie all of these foundational lessons into one activity, my dad invented the Cornetet National Bank. Instead of taking us to the bank down the street, he developed his own that was just for us kids. He was the CEO, so he set the hours, the terms, and the interest rates available to us. The Cornetet National Bank allowed my dad to directly teach us about the structure of a bank and how money systems work. At the same time, it gave us room to explore earning, spending, and saving in a truly hands-on way and allowed us to develop good habits around money years before we would need them as young adults.

The Cornetet National Bank was a very simple system, designed above all to be hands-on. My dad gave each of us a clear Tupperware container to serve as our vault. Each was labeled with our name on the lid, so there was Paige's National Bank and Brooke's National Bank first, and eventually Claire's and Peters' when they were old enough to join in. We all started with the National Bank at age five or six. When you were old enough to go to school, you were old enough to join the bank!

Because we were so little, the bank was only open one day per week: Saturday. After cleaning our rooms and zones, the very first Dad's Class lessons centered around the National Bank. Each Saturday, my dad handed us our allowance, which went right into the Tupperware box. This is also where we saved our earned money, and each week we could count it and watch it grow. When the bank closed for the week, the Tupperware boxes went on a high closet shelf to keep the money safe.

Dad also gave us each a special notebook and pen to use as our bank ledger. He taught us to write down the date and the amount we added to the bank each week. We kept a running tally of what we had saved, and each week we checked the math and tracked our savings as they grew.

It's worth pausing here to note why all of this works so well for little kids. First, we got to handle and count our own money, and the tangible lesson made the money real to us. We could watch it accumulate in the box as well as on paper, which connected abstract math concepts to real life. As always, the routine of weekly National Bank time reinforced the importance of keeping track of our money regularly and turned financial life into a normal part of regular life. By the time we were adults, balancing a checkbook and tracking our investments was just something we did.

Initially, the Cornetet National Bank was very much a deposit-only institution, as the first lessons were all about saving our money and watching it grow. After three months of weekly deposits, my dad introduced the concept of interest. He explained that since we didn't spend our money, the bank was going to pay us for keeping it there. We looked at our ledgers and told Dad the total, and he handed us a 10 percent bonus to add to our savings.

One of the reasons my dad decided to make his own bank instead of having us open a passbook savings account is because he knew that a bigger incentive to save would help solidify the concept much faster than getting a penny at a time from a traditional bank. The Cornetet National Bank had a 10 percent interest rate paid out every three months, so we quickly realized that saving our money had real benefits. (To this day, I wish I could invest in the Cornetet National Bank!) By making the interest rate a cool 10 percent, Dad also made his life a lot easier: to figure the amount, all he had to do was look at our total and bump the decimal over. Keeping things simple for us meant that we would stay engaged, and he would never find the National Bank too time-consuming to keep up with.

Eventually, Dad added the concept of spending to the National Bank. Now, after we added our allowance and any interest to the ledger and the Tupperware container, we were also given the option to take money out to spend. It's no accident that so many of our Saturday outings included trips to the bookstore, gift shop, or other places designed to separate a kid from their money. The opportunity to spend was an intentional part of the learning.

We were always allowed to spend our money. There was never any rule about a minimum balance at the National Bank, and no one ever policed what we bought. If Brooke wanted to buy twenty dollars of Gobstoppers and gummy bears, she could do that—as long as she could pay for it herself. Part of what made the family economy work is that my parents did not buy us extras. We knew that if we wanted something, we had to save up for it. We also got to talk to our parents about our thinking regularly. Each Saturday, the National Bank provided the opportunity for discussions about how our savings were doing, what we might spend the money on, whether those things would be worth it, and why. Basic banking concepts and lessons in value were built into the structure of our family life.

My dad also knew that each of his children would internalize the money lessons in a different way. He couldn't just talk about it once, and he knew that we would have to come to our own conclusions about earning, spending, and saving. I was a natural saver, and usually the reward of watching my balance increase was more satisfying to me than any single item I could buy. My sister Brooke, on the other hand, loved to spend her money, but she also didn't mind cleaning toilets and doing the work to earn more.

My dad told me recently that he knew we understood the concept one Saturday when Brooke tried to buy something at a small shop. The clerk told her the price, and Brooke realized she didn't have enough money with her to pay for it. She looked up at the clerk and said, "Okay, I'll be back. My bank only opens on Saturday, so I'll be back next week when I have the money."

She was six years old.

As we got older, the National Bank and our lessons about earning, savings, and spending evolved. Once we turned eight, we could do extra chores from the chore list to earn even more money. On Saturday mornings, we would add any wages from the week to our National Bank accounts as well. This was also true for any outside money we earned or that was given to us as a gift.

By high school, we transitioned from the Tupperware bins to a bank account with a debit card to make buying gas and snacks after school easier. We also needed a place to deposit checks from babysitting or other employment. This step made working with our money less concrete and more abstract, but by then, we had years of practice under our belts. We already knew how to track the balance and make sure we had enough money for the things we needed and wanted. We knew the importance of saving and what things were worth spending on.

By the time we went off to college, each Cornetet kid understood the basics of personal finance and had over a decade of practice managing their own money. And this was all thanks to the Saturdays we spent with a notebook and some Tupperware at the Cornetet Family Bank.

WHY ESTABLISHING A FAMILY BANK
IS IMPORTANT

The biggest reason to start a family bank and get a jump on teaching your kids the fundamentals of earning, spending and saving: they don't teach this in school, and it's fundamental for life!

While some high schools do have partnerships with local banks and may even have a small branch on campus for students, this is relatively rare—and just about nonexistent in elementary and middle schools. Many schools don't have the time or resources to provide deep teaching about personal finance, so the lessons they offer are often short enrichment activities. Your kids might get a few business-based word problems in math class, but that's about it.

I've heard from many parents over the years who wonder why this isn't taught in schools, but I would argue that parents should be the ones teaching their children about money. As we've seen in earlier chapters, money is a highly emotional topic, and it's very much a values issue. For example, your family budget is a values-based document. You decided what to spend money on and what to save up for, and these decisions demonstrate what you believe in. In many ways, your budget is the story of your family and what you find meaningful.

Do you really want someone else to have those conversations with your kids—the ones that help them learn what's important in life and what they should do with their money? My parents definitely didn't. Instead, the Cornetet National Bank provided sacred time for us to have conversations about money—and by extension, our family values—on an ongoing basis. By building a daily economy and bank from the ground up, my parents empowered each of us to write our own stories. We have each had a very different journey, but we were each completely prepared to handle our finances in a proactive, future-oriented way after our experiences with the Cornetet National Bank.

As a parent, you are the person best positioned to teach your children about money. Researchers have found that parents definitely do have an impact on their children's economic behavior, particularly when it comes to saving. When parents save, there is an increased likelihood that their children will save as adults.

Even more interesting is that parents have a strong impact on their children's future orientation, that is, their ability to delay gratification and think ahead about the consequences of their actions. Adults' ability to look to the future is hugely influenced by their childhood experiences at home, and a strong future orientation is correlated to everything from lower smoking rates to bigger savings account balances.[16]

---

[16] Paul Webley and Ellen K. Nyhus, "Parents' Influence on Children's Future Orientation and Saving," *Journal of Economic Psychology*, Vol. 27. 2006. 140–164, https://home.uia.no/ellenkn/WebleyNyhus2006.pdf.

This all makes sense, given that children are constantly observing their parents. If parents are saving, children will see that and learn from it—but only if it's out in the open. Having conversations about money in front of the children is the default way many people "teach" personal finance, but just think how much more powerful those lessons would be if they were intentionally directed at your children. When you include them in conversations around earning, saving, and spending, you ensure that you pass on good habits and answer all their questions directly.

You could accomplish a lot just by talking about money, but the real power of a family bank lies in the *doing*. By giving kids a chance to put the talk into practice, you're helping them learn and remember a very abstract concept in a concrete, hands-on way. If you've ever tried to answer an endless chain of "Why?" questions from a five-year-old, you know that explaining abstract concepts to a kid is really hard.

Young minds—and actually, all minds—work to make sense of concepts. As children's brains develop, they are constantly sorting new information into categories and looking for patterns to help create meaning. This work is much easier when children already have some background information to work with—or, as Christine Yount Jones puts it, a "mental hook" to hang new information on.[17] The best mental hooks are those that are tangible,

---

[17] Christine Yount Jones, "The Secret to Teaching Abstract Concepts to Kids," *Children's Ministry Magazine*. March 14, 2020, https://childrensministry.com/teaching-abstract-concepts/.

because they relate directly to sensory experiences. In other words, they are *real* in a way that the idea of money is not.

You could talk about the importance of saving money, or you could have your kids put their money in a real bank to show how it works. But when you let your child hold the money in their hand and watch it accumulate in that clear plastic box, you've created a true sensory experience. You've made banking real. Later in life, when it's time to move that money into a bank account and pay bills with an automatic transfer, the concept will already be in place. This is especially important as we move to an ever more cashless society. Money needs to feel real and meaningful, and young adults will need to have a solid sense of what it took to earn it, or they risk frittering it away into thin air because it feels so abstract.

It's the concrete nature of the Cornetet National Bank that made all those money lessons stick, and it's the reason why kids as young as five can begin to understand something as big as personal finance. When you make the lessons real, you're meeting young children at their developmental level.

HOW TO SET UP YOUR
OWN FAMILY BANK

I hope that the story of the Cornetet National Bank has inspired you to create your own family bank to teach your kids concrete lessons about earning, saving, and spending. This project should be fun, and it certainly doesn't have to be complicated. The basic elements are broken down into a few easy steps so you can do it yourself. I've also included some ideas for personalizing this project to align with your own values.

Step One: Start With the Vault

Introduce the concept of your family bank by creating a "vault" for each child. We used clear Tupperware boxes, and I do recommend something at least partially see-through to help your kids really see their savings accumulate. The container should be durable and fairly large so there's plenty of room to grow.

Beyond those basics, there's plenty of room to personalize the container, so let your kids label and decorate it in the way that will be most fun for them. You can use stickers, drawings, paint, or anything else that you have on hand. Personalizing the vault will help create ownership, and it's a great project for families that value creativity.

Step Two: Build and Track Savings

Once the bank is in business, your kids will need some money to put into it. My dad gave us an allowance based on our ages, and this was a base level of income that we didn't have to earn—he just wanted us to learn to save. You might decide to base an allowance on age, or you may prefer to start your kids off on equal footing, with the same amount of income. This is completely up to you and your family dynamic: Do you want to encourage a bit of competition and comparison about who can save more? If so, starting on a level playing field will be important. Do you want to offer regular raises, or would you prefer to keep allowances low to encourage more earning? There's no right or wrong answer here, but it's worth thinking through your system so it emphasizes your values.

Next, teach your kids to track their money in a bank account ledger. We did this with a simple spiral-bound notebook and pen to record the date, debits, and credits each week. The math was fairly simple at first, and you can check your kids' work if they need help in the beginning. These tools can also be personalized: a decorative notebook, a special pen, or even a real ledger can help set the mood. I do recommend doing physical writing, though—an app is a little too abstract for young minds to get the most out of the family bank, and using a calculator will rob your kids of valuable math practice!

Step Three: Add Interest Payments

Once your bank has been in operation for at least several weeks and your kids have mastered the basics of saving, it's time to teach the concept of interest. First, decide how often you'd like to provide this bonus: Monthly? Quarterly? It should be often enough to be rewarding but not so often that it doesn't feel special.

Next, decide on your interest rate. My dad picked 10 percent because it made the math very easy, and he could show us directly how our balance affected how much we earned in interest. You can choose to dial your interest higher or lower as you see fit. For older kids, you may even consider someday showing them how a prime rate changes and adjust their earnings accordingly.

Step Four: Provide Opportunities to Earn

Earning is one of the pillars of personal finance, so you don't want your kids to rely on the free ride of an allowance forever. If you haven't already established a chore list for your kids to earn extra money, consider doing that now. This is another activity that can be personalized to reflect your values. Are some jobs part of regular family life? If so, they should remain unpaid. Are other jobs paid because you dislike them, and do the prices you pay reflect the value of the work to you? For example, if you hate raking leaves, you could let your kids know that this is a service you are willing to pay extra for!

If you value entrepreneurship, you may instead encourage your kids to come up with their own business plan or job list. My dad valued negotiation skills, so he had us bid for the jobs once we got older, which introduced both competition as we sought to land the jobs and cooperation as we realized we could band together. If you value community, you could set up your jobs to be done as a group, with everyone earning payment together.

Step Five: Provide Opportunities to Spend

Finally, don't forget that taking money out of the bank is just as important as putting it in. Your kids will learn what the money is worth to them, and this is also a valuable hands-on lesson. Take them shopping, and discuss what things cost. On a regular basis, allow them to withdraw their money to buy the things they want. My dad did this weekly, but you can set up your family bank hours to best suit your schedule. I would caution that a cooling-off period during which the bank is closed will help your kids learn to delay gratification and hang on to more of their money. They might realize they don't want that video game that much, after all, if they have to wait a few days to get their hands on the money to pay for it!

It will be tempting to tell your children what to buy, and even more so, what not to buy. Don't do it! The best learning here will be from experience, and you have to let them make their own mistakes. You can relax knowing you've created very low-stakes conditions for them to experiment in, and if they blow all their money on the latest fad, they'll eventually learn to earn it back and do better in the future. Likewise, you need to resist the temptation to give them extra money or buy little gifts on the side. Once you have the family bank in place, your job is to provide for needs—your kids will learn to provide for their own wants.

Transform
Abstract
to Tactile

Make
Acts
Concrete

Parents
Have Major
Impact!

In this chapter, we learned how to create a family bank to teach the crucial financial lessons of earning, saving, and spending. Making these acts concrete helps children understand the highly abstract concepts of banking and personal finance. It also makes learning vivid and fun.

Research has shown that parents have a major impact on their children's financial learning, and those who work to demonstrate a future orientation set their kids up for success in the form of bigger savings. These financial lessons are also an important opportunity to pass your most important values on to your children by actions rather than just words.

Back in that gift shop, I spent so much time deciding if buying that wolf figurine was worth the money. I was only eight, but the thought process I went through is still with me. That outing—and the many more that followed—made me be more aware of my purchases and taught me to check myself: Why do I want this? What is this going to bring to me? These days, the purchases are much larger, and I know what I value. I'll spend on education and experiences, because I find these to be meaningful and have lasting value in my life. Wolf figurines, not so much.

The concept of the family bank is so simple to set up, but it's one of the most powerful learning tools I know of to teach kids about what it means to earn, save, and spend money. If you take away just one lesson from this book to try with your family, make it the family bank.

Even the best family bank will eventually leave your kids wishing they had more money. Saving can be slow, even with high parental interest rates. When your kids start to want more, it's time to teach them about investing.

6

SATURDAY MORNINGS

No one I've ever met grew up with a Saturday schedule quite like the one we had in the Cornetet house. While other kids were sleeping in or enjoying a bowl of sugary cereal while watching cartoons in their pajamas, we were already dressed, cleaning our rooms and zones, and tracking our saving and spending at the Cornetet National Bank.

And once those routines were complete, it was time for a reward. "Go grab your notebook," Dad announced. It was time to come to the table for Dad's Class.

Brooke and I each had our own notebook and pen that we used just for Dad's Class. We gathered at the table on the patio, which

Dad had set up as a cross between a boardroom and a classroom. He had an easel and chart paper ready to go, plus plenty of colored markers. We definitely got a taste of what it would be like to be in a work meeting with my dad thanks to the office supplies, but the "classroom" was also set up to be comfortable and fun. Being outside was way better than being stuck inside, like we would be at our regular school, and Dad always worked to find a hook that would make the lesson entertaining.

At the beginning of each class, Dad would write the title of the lesson at the top of the chart. That was our cue to start a new page in our notebooks. I still have mine, with each lesson clearly labeled at the top of the page and marked with the date for future reference.

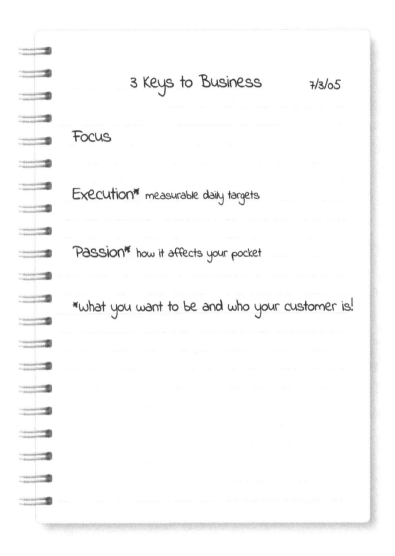

3 Keys to Business   7/3/05

Focus

Execution* measurable daily targets

Passion* how it affects your pocket

*what you want to be and who your customer is!

My dad is a very visual person and is a pretty great artist, so he often drew illustrations for us as he explained a financial concept. This might have included pie charts or other graphs to show money could grow exponentially or be used over time. As a kid, these visuals made tricky math concepts come to life.

Dad's Class was generally only about twenty minutes long, and there were never copious pages of notes. It was always just enough to present a concept and have us practice examples. When we learned about the Rule of 72, for example, we did the math to create a chart that showed how long it would take us to double our money at 7 percent, 10 percent, 12 percent, and 15 percent interest. We also made a chart calculating how much money we would have in the Cornetet National Bank if we let it continue compounding at 10 percent interest for our whole lives. This made the math personal and helped us visualize exactly what saving and investing could look like for us, which was very motivating. By eighth grade, I already had a roadmap for saving that showed me I could be a millionaire by the time I was sixty-five years old. I could do it!

DEVELOPING A LIFE SKILLS
CURRICULUM

My dad was a businessman who took over the family company from his grandfather. Business is in his blood. He's passionate about it and he's good at it. And when he became a father, he knew he wanted to pass everything he had learned on to his children, so that we could be just as successful in life as he was.

Since business was Dad's area of expertise, it's only natural that when he sat down to think about what he wanted to teach us, he ended up with a list of concepts squarely centered around money. From the time we were little, Dad was very intentional about teaching us financial life skills.

Many of these structures were established for us when we were in elementary school, including our family laws, chore lists, and the Cornetet National Bank. As we got older and shifted into middle and high school, my dad knew that what he taught us would also need to evolve. His Saturday morning classes were how he took our financial learning to the next level: the math got harder and the concepts more abstract.

Dad also added many specific business lessons to his personal curriculum for us. This was on purpose: he wanted to share what he knew and hopefully ignite a passion in us to start our own businesses. He also knew that many of the skills that helped him run a successful business would be important for us as we learned to deal with people, negotiate with others, and present ourselves as capable, responsible workers on the job. He approached lessons through the lens of a businessman, but he was really giving us a course in life skills.

Brooke and I took Dad's Class together as teenagers while Claire and Peter worked on more age-appropriate chores, since they were much younger. When Brooke and I graduated from Dad's

Class, Claire and Peter were just ready to begin. Our notebooks from this time were filled with topics like:

- The Number One Rule: Tithe 10 Percent

- The Rule of 72

- Passive Income

- The Stock Market

- Credit vs. Debit

- How the Bank Makes Money

- How to Hire Someone

- The Three Keys to Business

- What Customer Service Means

Once in a while, my mom took over class time to teach us her own lessons. Mom's Class was very different, because she had her own style of communication and areas of expertise, but it was equally valuable. Her professional background is in sales, so her lessons were all about interpersonal skills. For example, she taught us about posture and what it reveals about people's personalities and emotions. She was very focused on helping us figure out where people were coming from so we would know how to work with them effectively.

My parents approached teaching us differently, but their lessons had a few things in common. First, they focused on topics that they knew very well from their own professions. They also made sure to teach us things that weren't covered in school—at least not regularly. Finally, they had us take notes, which helped us remember the concepts and signaled that they were really important for us to remember. And that signal came across loud and clear because I still have my Dad's Class notebook with me today!

WHY DIRECTLY TEACHING YOUR CHILDREN LIFE SKILLS IS IMPORTANT

Ultimately, the point of Dad's Class was to make sure he had the time and space to pass on his personal wisdom. Families get busy, and my dad knew that if he wasn't intentional about developing a process for teaching us what he knew, it would never happen. In the process, making that sacred time helped strengthen family bonds and led us to a deeper understanding of my parents' beliefs and values.

Of course, those life skills also have a specific, direct benefit too. We learned how to do stuff! When you think about what it takes to survive in the world, there's so much that kids need to know when they finally step out on their own. Financial lessons are a huge part of that, but there are also plenty of other topics, like how to communicate with others, run a household, fix things when they break, keep your body healthy and fit—the list goes on.

Too often, families are seriously pressed for time. Parents work long hours, and kids are running from one activity to the next. Life skills tend to get lost in the shuffle. It's easy to assume that kids will just pick up the basics by observation or osmosis, but that's not enough to ensure that they're ready to apply these important skills.

Take, for example, the college freshman living on her own for the first time. When she runs out of clean clothes, will she know what to do when she gets into the laundry room and faces that coin-operated machine? Laundry isn't something you learn how to do by watching a parent do endless loads. Someone has to show you how!

Lots of college freshmen get a quick crash course in laundry right before they move out, but that's not a workable strategy for covering all the life skills your kids will need to know. If you want your kids to know how to do something, you have to teach them—directly and intentionally.

And let's be real: that teaching takes work. When I look back at my Dad's Class notebook, I can see that behind each lesson was a planning session and serious thought about how to break down a complex topic for a kid to understand. Each one of those lessons took a major investment of time and energy to design and then to execute on a Saturday morning. Intentional parenting takes time, effort, and real commitment to create the structures and routines that make learning possible.

Direct teaching of life skills also allows you to hedge your bets as a parent. You might invest in piano lessons, sports camps, and private math tutoring only to find out that your child develops an intense interest in writing poetry. You can't predict what specific skills your kids will need as they grow and develop their own passions. But you *can* make sure they understand the basics of running a household, handling their money, interacting with others, and putting in an honest day's work—skills that will translate into every kids' future.

Finally, by teaching your children life skills, you're also taking the time to impart your wisdom to them. You've learned a lot by experience, and one of the most important things we do as humans is pass on what we know. All the lessons and advice from my Dad's Class didn't just come from him. So much of it was also passed down from my grandfather and my great-grandfather. There are four generations' worth of lessons for me to work from when I start my own class with my future children. That's an incredible connection to family across time that grounds me in a real sense of who I am, and I can't wait to pass that powerful, grounding wisdom on to my own children.

For us, the family business is what ties all those lessons together. You don't need to be a business owner to have your wisdom benefit your children. You have the power and the knowledge to teach them what you know and what you believe, and what you have learned from your parents and grandparents before you. We all have stories, good and bad, to learn from. The trick is to be intentional about passing it on.

HOW YOU CAN CREATE YOUR OWN CLASS

The first thing to know about designing your own Mom's Class or Dad's Class is that you are in charge. Your classes should be a reflection of *you*: your values, your skills, and your interests. My dad designed his classes around important money and business lessons, but that doesn't mean that you have to do the same thing. Saturday mornings can be about whatever you want your kids to learn.

Step One: Brainstorm Ideas for Lessons

Maybe you're a college professor, and you want to teach your kids about your academic passion or how to design and fund a research project. Maybe you're a doctor or nurse and want to teach your kids first aid or good health. Maybe you're an avid gardener who wants to teach your children to grow their own food. It's all up to you to decide which aspects of your life are the most meaningful to share with your family.

To get started, I recommend a good old-fashioned brain dump.

1. Start by listing all of the life skills you want your children to learn.

2. Next, consider the skills and knowledge you use at work. What are some things you could teach your children about what you do and how you do it?

3. What pastimes and hobbies could you share? Consider breaking down big concepts into small lessons, like planting a seed or pitching a tent.

4. Take a moment to review your thinking about family values. Do any specific lessons or topics come to mind that would reinforce your values? List them here.

5. Now, take a look back at your answers to the first four questions. Why is each of these important? What makes them worth passing on? You can write your answer next to each idea, or you can just think about it.

6. Finally, place a star by the lessons that are most important to you and that feel doable right now (i.e., they are age appropriate for your kids and you feel confident in teaching them).

Step Two: Create a Class Schedule

In my family, Dad's Class was on a Saturday morning because that's the time we had set aside to spend together as a family. You might prefer to have class on Friday nights before pizza and games, or on a Sunday afternoon. It could be Wednesday after school if that's what works best for you!

The day and time isn't important, but consistency is key. Take a hard look at your family's schedule to choose the best time, and then make that time sacred. Even if you can only commit to every other week or once per month, make sure you stick to the plan. This is crucial to show your kids that it matters.

As you schedule, keep in mind that these classes are meant to be short and sweet! Your lessons shouldn't be more than about twenty minutes for younger kids and possibly 30 for older ones. This will keep your kids engaged and make the whole structure more doable for everyone.

Finally, you'll need to carve out a little lesson planning time in your own schedule so you can be ready to teach your class. This will likely take about an hour as you think about how you'll teach the lesson and gather any materials or props you'll need to do it. You'll also want to summarize the main points and leave a bit of time to reflect on how the lesson went.

Step Three: Create Your Classroom

We always had class at the patio table, which provided a nice work surface but had the benefit of being outside. It's a good idea to have class in a consistent location, and you'll want to choose an area that meets your needs. If you plan to do a lot of art projects, choose a place where you can be messy. You'll also want to make sure you have good lighting and space to work, and that you and your family enjoy gathering there.

As you plan where to meet, you'll also need to think about what supplies you will need. Your materials will vary by lesson, but you might always want to have a whiteboard or easel and chart paper. You'll also want a place to keep basics like notebooks, pens, markers, and other tools you plan to use regularly. It's also a good idea to limit distractions, so consider leaving tablets and smartphones in a drawer.

Step Four: Plan Your Lesson

Each week, refer back to your big brainstorming list and pick one lesson that you're excited to teach. It doesn't matter what you choose, since they're all important, and you have plenty of time to get to all of them. In the beginning, it makes sense to choose topics that feel easy to you: easy to teach, easy to explain, easy to set up and clean up. You want some wins right out of the gate!

Planning the lesson doesn't have to be hard. Start by naming your topic, and then ask yourself what you want your kids to know about it. How will you explain it so they can understand? It's a good idea to think about this ahead of time, at least in general terms.

Next, what kind of activity can you do together to show the concept in action? For my dad's financial lessons, we did some math problems and discussed what the ideas meant for our own money. You might be able to build or make something, do a role play, do some creative writing, or play a game. The key is to add a hands-on element to make the lesson memorable and *fun*.

If you're not sure how to go about teaching a certain topic to your kids, don't stress—that's what the internet is for! I guarantee that someone has already figured out a way to teach that concept to a child and has put an idea or lesson plan on the internet. Just Google a topic to see what's out there. Pinterest, YouTube, and parenting websites are good places to find kid-friendly ideas, and the website Teachers Pay Teachers often has great worksheets, lesson plans, and activities on a whole range of topics if you're having trouble designing your own. There's no pressure to reinvent the wheel here.

It's also a good idea to create a short list of low-prep lessons to use in a pinch. If you're having a very busy week, these are things that you can teach that take little to no effort on your part but are still meaningful. I would fall back on personality and strengths assessments, since this is part of what I do for a living. These are usually fun for kids to do and provide plenty of fodder for discussion, and all you have to do is pull it up on a website. Other good ideas for quick lessons are "how-to" days: how to make an omelet, how to use a toilet plunger, how to iron a shirt—the list is nearly endless.

Finally, a word about those financial life skill lessons. If teaching your children about investing and business topics made your list of lessons to teach, but you're not sure how to get started, that's okay. I've developed a set of resources to help you cover the top ten financial themes that every kid should understand before they head to college:

- Understanding compound interest

- Investing in stocks

- Generating passive income

- Managing expenses

- Understanding customer service

- Generating business ideas

- Establishing and achieving goals

- Automating and delegating tasks

- Paying for college

- Understanding debit vs. credit

You can access these lessons for free at MyDadsClass.com.

KEY TAKEAWAYS

In this chapter, we learned that many of the most important life skills are not taught in school. If you as the parent don't teach them, no one else will. It's also not enough to hope that children learn these lessons by watching you. Instead, they need direct instruction and engaging, hands-on practice.

When you intentionally plan and deliver lessons about the life skills you value, you're sharing generational wisdom with your children. You're also carving out time and space to share quality time together. When you're intentional about building a Saturday around these principles, you'll find that you're actually building a whole life around your values—and passing them on to your children.

Of all the things my parents did for us, the time we spent together in Dad's Class had the greatest impact on my life. I learned so much during that time, and if my parents hadn't taught it to me,

I would have had to figure it out the hard way. And when it comes to money, learning the hard way can have lifetime repercussions. I was truly blessed to enter adulthood with a whole range of skills that set me up for success.

Beyond those specific life skills, I also learned the importance of being intentional about your life. Making the time to meet with us showed how important we were to my dad. We were worth his time and effort. As an adult, I understand that when you care about something, you need to place your focus on it and nurture it, whether it's your career, your partner, or your child—or all three! Dad's Class also modeled that type of integrity and commitment to me, and for that, I am forever grateful.

While parents are definitely their children's most powerful teachers, you don't have to go it alone when it comes to teaching financial and life skills. Other people in your life can be great adjunct instructors as well.

7

HARD STRUCTURE MEETINGS

One summer morning when I was twelve or thirteen, I remember waking up early to go to a meeting. We had family meetings and Dad's Class all the time, of course, but this was different. For this meeting, Brooke and I had to dress up in our best approximation of professional attire.

Being in our early teens, this wasn't easy. I didn't exactly have a closet full of power suits to choose from, so I went with a Sunday dress and shoes. We ate early and got into the car with Dad for the short drive to his stock broker's office. Brooke and I glanced at each other in the back seat, and I could tell that she felt just as uncomfortable as I did.

When we arrived, the office was cool, and the secretary greeted us just as if we were adults. "Can I get you anything, Miss? Coffee or water?" Even though we were thirsty, Brooke and I said no. We were too embarrassed to let this very nice lady wait on us—we were just kids, and we knew we were out of place in this fancy office.

We were led into a cavernous room with a long, polished conference table. The stockbroker came in his suit and tie and shook hands with my dad. We had to shake hands firmly as well, though at least I knew what to do here—we had practiced greeting adults with a firm handshake in Dad's Class before.

The stockbroker invited us to sit down as he organized his stack of papers at the head of the table. He handed each of us a spiral-bound notebook filled with colorful charts and graphs.

I had no idea what I was looking at.

Dad and his stockbroker went through the portfolio page by page, reviewing the performance of each of the family's investments. Honestly, it felt like they were speaking a foreign language. When the stockbroker asked if we had any questions, Brooke and I just shook our heads. We had nothing at all to add to the conversation.

But Dad definitely did. We weren't exactly sure what he was talking about, but we could tell from the way the stockbroker responded that Dad was asking important questions. The two of them had a good rapport and clearly respected each other as equals. They worked together to make decisions about the investments for the future, and eventually the meeting ended.

After that Dad took us to McDonald's for an ice cream cone—and a mini Dad's Class to debrief about the meeting we had just witnessed. He explained that part of what we looked at in all those charts and graphs was the share of McDonald's that our family owned.

We owned part of the McDonald's in town? That was news to us!

Dad explained how shares worked and that every quarter the McDonald's company would pay us a dividend as our small percentage of what all the McDonald's in the world earned. "You're an owner of this company, and you just used the money you earned from it to buy the ice cream here," he said.

This hit me like a flash. "So the ice cream is free?" I asked.

"Well, you earned the money for it," Dad explained. "And you did it not by working at McDonald's but by investing in it."

If I ever had an aha moment about money, this was it. I could earn money without working *in the real world*. It wasn't just the Cornetet National Bank that would pay me, but real companies. And they were everywhere I looked, since Dad pointed out that we owned stock in BP when we filled our gas tank and in Walgreens, where we picked up some toothpaste on our way home.

Just like I was with the gold coins, I was hooked on this concept. The next time I got to go to a meeting with the stockbroker, I would try harder to pay attention. After all, these were *my* companies, too.

INTRODUCING KIDS TO OTHER PROFESSIONALS

Throughout their financial lives, your children will eventually have to work with many professionals: accountants, lawyers, financial advisers, insurance brokers, and more. Introducing your older kids and teenagers to these professionals will help them understand their roles and the main concepts of their industries. In addition to direct financial lessons, you'll also help your children gain the soft skills necessary to get the most out of these crucial relationships.

As a businessman, my dad has always worked with many other professionals to manage his finances. He understood the importance of working closely with experts to make the most of his money—and his time. My dad was brilliant, and part of his brilliance was knowing he couldn't do everything himself. So he developed a set of trusted advisers with whom he maintained long-term relationships.

So by the time we were in middle and high school, my dad made sure that we sat in on what he called his "hard structure meetings." These were with his accountant at tax time, his stockbroker for quarterly portfolio reviews, and his lawyer whenever an issue came up.

My dad had several goals in bringing us to these meetings. First, he wanted us to get a sense of what a professional meeting looked and felt like. That's why we had to dress up, get there on time, and shake hands with everyone in the room. We learned the basics of polite conversation and body language through this real-world practice, which was a lot different than just talking about it at dinner or practicing a handshake at home!

Second, he wanted us to learn about the ins and outs of the financial world. When we met with the stockbroker, we got a lesson on the stock market and what it meant to earn dividends. Eventually, he used those meetings to explain the difference between stocks, bonds, and other investments. When we met with the accountant, we got lessons on how those investments were taxed, how deductions worked, and eventually how to file our own income tax return.

These meetings often functioned like field trips for Dad's Class. Attending them let us see things in action, but afterward, he always took the time to explain what we were witnessing. These meetings provided context, and my dad was always great at creating examples that had to do with our everyday lives.

Finally, attending hard structure meetings provided valuable role modeling for adult life. I remember being amazed that my dad could talk to these people and be so confident in asking them questions. He also made suggestions to them, and he wasn't afraid to say what he wanted. Watching my dad in these meetings showed us that it's okay to ask questions, and we should never leave anything unsaid when it comes to our money. It also gave us the confidence that, someday, we could do it too.

WHY HARD STRUCTURE MEETINGS ARE IMPORTANT

One of the most valuable lessons I learned from attending hard structure meetings is that expertise is important. I got a look at whole systems of finance and how they worked, and that helped me understand my place in the system—including the fact that I am not an expert on things like taxes or inheritance law. Working with a professional on these issues is worth the fee to prevent problems down the road.

In my family, this lesson was made crystal clear by my great-grandmother. For years and years, she never wanted to hire a lawyer to set up a trust for her heirs. She didn't think it was necessary, didn't want to bother—and, if we're being honest, probably had a hard time thinking about dying. Shortly before she died, however, she had a change of heart and quickly set up a trust.

Unfortunately, that trust wasn't done well, and that money has been sitting in Michigan for generations. My dad pays Michigan taxes on it every year, but the cost to remove the assets is greater than the amount of money in the trust.

This is definitely not what my great-grandmother would have wanted, and my dad tells this story—a *lot*—to underline how important it is to get these jobs done well. This is especially true for life's big transitions: marriage, the birth of children, and death. If you aren't already working with a few good professionals like a tax advisor, investment advisor, and a lawyer for your wills and trusts, please take it from my family: this is well worth it for your financial future, and not just so you can invite your kids along for the ride!

I can't help but wonder how things might have been different if my great-grandmother had more experience working with a lawyer and asking questions about what she didn't understand. Would she have gotten the trust done sooner rather than rushed into a mistake? Would she have had the confidence to ask all the important questions instead of just going along with what was presented to her?

Giving your older kids and teens the opportunity to get comfortable with these meetings goes a long way toward building their confidence. My dad made it clear that there was no such thing as a dumb question, so we always felt like we could ask about anything that happened in those meetings. We started by asking Dad, but as we got older, we also gained the confidence to ask questions directly to those professionals. I know some people in their forties and fifties who are afraid to ask their financial advisers really important questions because they're afraid of looking dumb. If they had been empowered to work with these professionals earlier in their lives, they would be able to do so with confidence now.

In his biography of Steve Jobs, Walter Isaacson describes how the computer mogul brought his son Reed to the office with him. "I'm going to be in meetings 24/7 for probably two days and I want you to be in every single one because you'll learn more in those two days than you would in two years at business school."[18]

This type of learning is two-fold. First, there's the big-picture learning by osmosis that comes just from seeing adults in action. How do they relate to each other? What do adult relationships look like? This is something that kids don't learn in school, because they are largely interacting with each other or with a teacher. Because school is necessarily a kid-centered place, there aren't many opportunities to observe adults in action. You'll have to be intentional about providing opportunities for these types of interactions.

The second type of learning that I suspect Steve Jobs wanted to provide for his son was a set of specific soft skills that are required

---

[18] Walter Isaacson, *Steve Jobs* (New York: Simon & Schuster, 2011).

to make adult interactions successful. These include things like active listening, expressing opinions respectfully, asking good questions, and learning the languages required in different situations.

Those languages include both body language and specific words and phrases. You don't, for example, wear sweatpants and put your head down on the conference table in a business meeting. Every industry also has its own lingo, so accountants will sometimes quite literally speak differently than doctors, lawyers, and even teachers. When you expose your kids early to those different ways of speaking and behaving, it makes it easier for them to pick up new jargon and feel comfortable with it.

Of course, hard structure meetings are also ideal for helping your teens transition into young adulthood. Even after watching my dad work with his accountant for years, I still needed the experience of doing it on my own, with my own money on the line. Once I started working, my dad would set up a meeting with me and his accountant to go over my personal income and what that would mean for my taxes. How much did I make this year? What tax bracket did that put me in? Was there anything I could write off? Working through it, step by step, taught me a lot about how taxes work and how to plan ahead—and it all became much more concrete when I was actually talking about my own money. By the time I was ready to start my own business, I had a huge head start on the background knowledge I needed to ensure its success!

Finally, you never know when your hard structure meetings will inspire a child to explore new interests and potential careers. It's hard for many kids to connect the subjects they learn in school to real job possibilities, but seeing those jobs in action can make all the difference. For me, developing a relationship with my family's accountant provided a real-life work opportunity as well. This experience led directly to me becoming a licensed financial planner, and it all started with one of those hard structure meetings I went to as an awkward middle schooler. Hard structure meetings can provide a meaningful avenue for self-discovery in addition to specific skills and knowledge.

HOW TO GET YOUR KIDS INVOLVED IN HARD STRUCTURE MEETINGS

Bringing your kids along to a meeting with your accountant or banker can be as easy as packing them into the car and having them come along. But you'll get better outcomes if you take a more thoughtful approach.

Consider your answers to the following questions.

1. What "hard structure" meetings do you already do regularly?

2. Think about your line of work. What types of meetings do you have regularly? What types of people do you meet with on the job?

3. Think about your personal network of family and friends. Are any of them experts in a life skill you'd like to teach your child? List them here to round out your options.

4. Take a look at the ideas you've come up with above. Which of these meetings feel like they could be beneficial for your children to see? Which are the most age appropriate?

If these questions were difficult for you, that's okay. Not everybody has connections to financial professionals. In this case, you can turn making that first meeting into a learning project for the whole family. If you need to start from scratch, I recommend reaching out to a tax preparer first. You know what they say about death and taxes, so *everyone* can benefit from a consultation. And if that doesn't feel doable for you, open up your tax software and walk your kids through the process of doing a 1040-EZ for themselves.

You can also consider a meeting with a financial planner or even your local bank to discuss some investment options. An initial consultation should be low-key if you're not ready to commit to any investment, and it will give you plenty of fodder for conversations with your kids.

For those conversations to be fruitful, it's a good idea to plan ahead. Use this chart to organize your thinking about each hard structure meeting you might take your kids to.

Hard Structure Meetings with _____

What Kids Should Know Ahead of Time	Topics and Concepts to Explain Afterwards	Soft Skills to Explore Afterwards

For example, you might want your kids to know that the lawyer's office is in a skyscraper and tends to be very cold and quiet, and that they will need to speak softly and wear "hard pants" instead of sweats. You might list some big ideas that your lawyer will mention, like what a deed is and how wills work so you can be prepared to explain it afterward—or to ask your lawyer to explain it on the spot. Finally, think about the soft skills that might come up during the meeting, such as how to show active listening, shake hands, and thank people for their help.

All of these will make for a great discussion after the meeting. Don't skip this step! I recommend having the conversation over ice cream to make it more fun, but you can also use this list—and anything interesting that pops up during the course of the meeting—as fodder for future lessons in your Mom's or Dad's Class, too.

In this chapter, we learned that older kids and teens can gain knowledge about how financial systems work when they're invited to meet with professionals and observe them in action. Having your children experience hard structure meetings helps them understand more complex financial education topics while providing a glimpse of how adults interact with each other in the real world. These meetings also give kids a chance to hone the soft skills of active listening and appropriate questioning to build confidence in their ability to work with adults in many different fields.

Many people assume that kids can't understand things about the adult world, but this attitude shortchanges young people by keeping them out of important conversations. By the time your child is eight years old, they're ready to start talking about taxes, investing, and other real-world topics to build a foundation for deeper understanding.

In my own life, those early meetings definitely put me on the path to feeling confident in working with accountants and other professionals in my own business. I learned to ask questions early, and I'm still asking them. I recently met a podcaster who told me how she claims all of her hair and makeup expenses as a business deduction because she has to look a certain way for her work. Is that true? Can I do that? I won't hesitate to ask my accountant about it in our next meeting, if it does seem a little silly.

Likewise, I'm also entering my thirties well ahead of the game when it comes to investing and saving for retirement. I began learning the lingo of personal finance in middle school, so now I'm fluent in the language of 401(k)s and capital gains taxes in a way that many of my friends are not. That means I have a good extra decade of confident saving and planning under my belt, which has set me up to thrive in whatever kind of future awaits. And for that I'm super grateful, even though, at the time, I would rather not have been dressed up on a Saturday morning.

Hard structure meetings offer kids a taste of adulthood, but eventually, your kids will need more structured experiences that prepare them to choose a career and live independently.

8

EXPERIENCES WITH
COMPANIES

Throughout my childhood, I attended a Montessori school that emphasized hands-on learning. I was lucky in that my school didn't stop at sixth grade but instead offered an extra two years of middle school curriculum. Though we were no longer doing math with blocks and measuring cups, the school was completely committed to providing real-world experiences.

In seventh and eighth grade, this came in the form of a self-designed internship with local companies. We had to decide on a career we were interested in and contact the company and ask about shadowing an employee. Then we had to do a one-week apprenticeship where we spent five full days on the job.

I loved theater and performing, and I especially loved putting on costumes to do it—I still love the way putting on a costume lets you try on a whole new personality in an instant. So I knew exactly what I wanted to do. I called the Golden Apple Theatre in Sarasota, Florida, and set up an internship in the costume department.

I was twelve, and I was getting in on the ground floor at the theater. I was psyched!

On Monday morning, I walked in the doors and was led backstage to the costume shop. The lady with whom I was apprenticing clapped her hands together and said, "Okay, today is wash day!"

She showed me a gigantic pile of costumes: ball gowns, army uniforms, dresses, and suits from all different time periods. And they were all dirty.

I spent the day camped out alone in front of the giant washer and dryer, moving clothes from one to the other. Because many of the costumes had a lot of fabric, I could only put a few in at a time. I must have done ten loads of laundry that day, with just a short break for lunch.

I had never been so bored in my life.

During that week, I learned other things about costuming for the theater, of course. I watched the costume mistress whip together a new wimple for one of the nuns in *Sister Act* and rush it to her backstage just before she went on. I learned to sort clothing by era and figure out how to safely store costumes between performances. But the biggest lesson I learned that week was this: I did *not* want to be a costume designer.

PROVIDING HANDS-ON LEARNING EXPERIENCES

In the first chapter of this book, one of the major tenets of Montessori education is that teachers must give as much to the hands as they do to the eyes—that is, children learn best when they are provided hands-on experiences. Manipulating objects and practicing skills helps solidify lessons through repetition, but as kids get older, practical experiences also help them decide what to focus on: what they love, what they're good at, and what they can see themselves doing for a career.

My dad was committed to Montessori education specifically because of this hands-on approach, and if the school hadn't provided apprenticeships in middle school, I'm sure he would have found a way to have us seek out those work experiences on our own, perhaps as a natural extension of our hard structure meetings.

As it was, the apprenticeships allowed students total freedom to choose what we wanted to explore. This is crucial, because it gave us ownership of the project and empowered us to follow our own interests. For many kids, it's hard to connect the dots between a school subject and a career, but this opportunity lets kids think about the job instead of just an academic subject.

To set up the apprenticeship, we had to contact the company and present a proposal, which required us to put many real-world skills into action: organization, writing, speaking, and negotiation. While we shadowed the person on the job, we learned not just about the job itself but also how businesses operate and, for me anyway, how to handle the boredom of day-to-day tasks.

During the week of the apprenticeship, my parents spent a good deal of time debriefing me about the day. We talked about the tasks, how people behaved, and how I felt about the work. This crucial conversation helped me put the experience in perspective. I knew right away that I didn't really like the costume shop, but it took deeper thinking and discussion to help me understand *why*. I loved costumes, but working alone at repetitive tasks was definitely not for me.

The school also required a written report about the apprenticeship, and between the conversations with my parents and the act of writing about my experience, I walked away with more than just insight about the job. I also gained a deeper understanding of myself as a person: what I liked, what I was good at, and what I wanted to focus on in the future.

As we got older, our experiences with companies also included summer jobs. My parents always wanted us to get out there and work, to experience what it was like to manage our time and our relationships with bosses and coworkers. For example, my dad set my brother Peter up with a summer job on his friend's farm, which was very much an experience in manual labor. Peter also tried his hand at manufacturing, and we all had experiences in customer service, whether it was selling cookies or keeping parents informed about how their children behaved after a night of babysitting. My sister Claire even started her own business selling custom-designed sweatshirts, which provided valuable lessons in sales, marketing, and supply and demand.

Looking back, these separate experiences added up to a well-rounded education in how businesses function. Farming and manufacturing work, and even my backstage apprenticeship, provided insight into where things come from and how they are made. Working in a shop or providing a service taught us how businesses operate to get people what they need. And of course, every job has an element of customer service and human interaction that teaches critical interpersonal skills. By providing us a taste of each, my parents made sure that we had a better understanding of our options beyond just academics as we prepared to go to college and choose a career.

WHY EXPERIENCES WITH COMPANIES
ARE IMPORTANT

During my internship, I quickly learned that having an interest in something is not the same as being suited to do it day in and day out. I loved costumes, but I needed to be with people instead of washing machines. My husband told me the story of his first job, which was laying sod for a landscaping company. When I asked him what he learned, he quickly responded, "That I didn't want to do physical work for my job." That's an important insight that steered him toward college and law school. Without trying different things, kids won't know what they like—or what they don't. The opportunity for self-discovery is what experiences with different companies is all about, even if those apprenticeships don't connect directly to a career. The more experience you have early on, the easier it is to find the right path later.

In college, my roommates were both planning to go into teaching. They took all the required courses and did well in them, but when their student-teaching semester finally came in their senior year, they were shocked to discover that they didn't actually like being in the classroom. It was a "Now what?" moment that came pretty late in the game. Imagine if they had been able to work in a classroom setting during freshman year to get a feel for what teaching was really like. If your child names an interest in a particular career, helping them experience it as soon as they can—whether by shadowing a friend for a day, getting a related summer job, or finding a more formal apprenticeship—will provide hands-on learning about the work and about themselves before you invest $200,000 on a degree in that field.

Having as many work experiences as possible also helps kids to understand what they're looking for in a work environment. Do they prefer quiet and calm, or are they energized by having lots of people around? Do they like working with their hands? Would they rather be outside or inside? What provides a sense of accomplishment, and what is so deadly boring that they'd rather scrub toilets?

As a parent, you can guide your child to be reflective about their apprenticeships to help them get the most out of their work experiences. Whether your child loves or hates their time at a company, be sure to ask some probing questions about *why* they feel that way. Kids may have trouble articulating their feelings at first, and this is where having many experiences will provide points of comparison to help them zero in on their preferences and talents.

As kids explore different jobs to understand what they might like, they're also beginning to master the basic soft skills required by every job. In his book *Outliers: The Story of Success,* Malcolm Gladwell talks about the 10,000 Hour Rule: in order to master any skill, a person needs to practice it for about 10,000 hours.[19] It

---

[19] Malcolm Gladwell, *Outliers: The Story of Success* (New York: Little, Brown and Company, 2008).

takes a long time to get good at something, whether you become a doctor, teacher, or an electrician. Your child might not need to master scooping popcorn at the movie theater for a future career, but they do need to master plenty of soft skills involved in the work: organizing tasks, accepting feedback, working with others, managing busy periods, and more. In a paid job, your child will also begin to master some basics of adulthood, like filling out an application, tax forms and setting up direct deposit for their paychecks. These may sound small, but these skills also take time to master, and giving your child a head start will take some of the pressure off later. With soft skills already under their belt, they can focus more intently on the hard skills in their chosen career when the time comes.

Finally, one of the most important benefits of apprenticeships and work experiences is that they give kids a way to shine that goes beyond academics. In my family, academics were important, but we also learned that school wasn't everything. Being smart didn't necessarily make you a good person or a good worker. My dad struggled with reading the whole time he was in school. When he was a senior in high school, he finally asked his mother for reading lessons. She was shocked to discover that my dad had been getting by on memorizing and other strengths like storytelling and interpersonal relationships.[20]

---

[20] Kate Griggs, "5 Reasons Why Dyslexics Make Great Entrepreneurs," *LinkedIn,* July 6, 2020, https://www.linkedin.com/pulse/5-reasons-why-dyslexics-make-great-entrepreneurs-kate-griggs/.

He did get those lessons, and he's an avid reader now, but my dad's success in life was never based in academics. He never finished college, and instead learned the family business on the job. My mom was always on the lookout for ways to help us with learning differences, whether altering the seating arrangement to deal with "the wiggles" or providing lots of opportunities to shine outside of the classroom.

So many kids have amazing skills that aren't measured on standardized tests, and they can end up feeling like they're not smart or talented simply because they spend most of their time in a place where their natural abilities aren't valued. As a parent, you can be intentional about filling in those gaps to make sure your child feels successful and gets the opportunity to develop their full human potential. There's a world out there beyond school, so listen to your child's interests and encourage them to find experiences with companies that open their eyes to all the possibilities for the future.

HOW TO PROVIDE EXPERIENCES
WITH COMPANIES

There's a growing industry devoted to providing teens and young adults with internships, but you don't have to sign up for an expensive summer program to provide your child with valuable experiences with companies. In fact, shorter, more personalized experiences that you create with your child will provide more opportunities for learning than many generic internships that use students as glorified Starbucks runners.

Step One: Build a Wish List of Skills

The whole point of experiences with companies is to build a set of skills that will be useful in life. Some of these skills are specifically related to a particular field, such as learning to wait tables or operate a cash register. Other skills apply to a wide range of careers, such as time management and customer service. A third set of skills involves self-assessment about personal strengths and passions, such as a love of working outdoors or a desire to work with people.

So what do you want your child to get out of their experiences with companies? List your thoughts here (I've added some ideas to get you started!):

Hard Skills	Soft Skills	Self-Discovery
• Working at a bank to learn about money and numbers	• Waiting tables to learn about customer service	• Take Clifton Strength Finders Assessment

Next, take a moment to reflect on your own education and work experiences. What do you wish you had known or experienced before starting your career: a second language? Bookkeeping? The importance of comfortable shoes? Add these ideas to the wish list above.

Step Two: Brainstorm Opportunities

Answer the questions below to begin building a list of potential company experiences you can find or create for your child.

1. How can you use your own employment as an experience for your child? Consider ways to bring your child to work, have them shadow you, sit in on a Zoom call, etc.

2. Are there other opportunities for apprenticeship or shadowing within your company? Consider coworkers with different functions, other departments, summer jobs, and volunteering, or other existing opportunities for young people.

3. Think beyond your own employment to your network. What jobs do friends and family have that might be of interest to your child? List them here.

4. What work experiences would your child be most interested in? Be sure to include your child in the discussion— their answers may surprise you!

Step Three: Build Unique Experiences

Now it's time to take the skills you've identified and the opportunities available to you to create specific experiences for your child. Take a moment to review the skills you listed in Step One. Place a star by the ones that are most important.

Then think about which work opportunities will best teach those skills. You can organize your thoughts in the chart below:

Desired Skill	Potential Work Experiences

As you review what you wrote, you should be able to see which company experiences offer the best chance to explore the skills that are most important to you. Make these your priority, and get the ball rolling to set your child up with that experience. You may have to engage your network or create a proposal at your own workplace, or you might be able to take a more casual approach, depending on your office's policies.

In designing an apprenticeship, you should have two top priorities. First, get your child involved in the proposal: calling the company, asking for the opportunity, and designing their day are all great work skills in their own right. This will also help ensure the apprenticeship is of interest to your child.

Second, keep in mind that a short, intense apprenticeship or shadowing assignment is often more useful than months-long internships. Most companies aren't actually equipped to provide an educational experience for long-term interns, so they end up being under-utilized gofers. By creating your own experience, you can be far more intentional about the tasks your child will be doing and learning, which will ultimately lead to a richer experience.

KEY TAKEAWAYS

Get Your Child Involved

Create Hands-on Experiences

Learn What They DON'T Want to Do

In this chapter, we learned that hands-on experiences in the workplace provide a wealth of learning opportunities for older kids and teens. Whether they participate in a short apprenticeship, internship, or summer job, experiences with companies teach kids a variety of important skills, including the soft skills needed across many jobs. Experiences with companies also offer significant opportunities for self-discovery that aren't always possible in an academic setting.

Experiences with companies also help kids begin the process of leaving the nest. At some point, parents just cannot do all the teaching for the children anymore—nor should they. You can leverage the full community—including friends, family, religious and professional networks—to expand your child's world and provide the learning they need to succeed later in life.

In my own life, work experiences showed me what I didn't want to do and also pointed me toward my best talents. Obviously, a career in the arts wasn't for me. But my favorite summer job was being a camp counselor in a cabin of twelve girls. It was a 24/7 job, and that part was exhausting. But I was also able to express my full personality with those girls and use my talents of quick thinking and flexibility to harness the flow of their energy throughout the day. A lot of camp was making things up as you went along and selling it to the kids, and I loved that.

Fast-forward to today, and I finally have a career that lets me use that exact skill. In my business, I work with groups of people to help them discover their skills and talents—work that's not so different from being a camp counselor at times! I also find myself adjusting presentations at the last minute and thinking on the fly about how to best engage groups. My early work experiences showed me that I thrive in this type of environment and helped me hone the soft skills I would need as an entrepreneur. Carefully crafted experiences with companies can give your child that type of head start too.

Specific skills are just part of the recipe for a successful life. Work is only part of the picture. You'll also need to impart your hard-won wisdom for *living*.

9

SHARING WISDOM
ACROSS GENERATIONS

W hen I was little, my favorite food was corn on the cob. There was nothing as delicious as the sweet summer corn that Michigan farmers sold all through August. I remember juicy, golden ears piled high on a platter, and we could have as many as we wanted. Corn on the cob didn't last forever, so we ate as much as we could while it was in season.

In fact, my family often turned eating ears of corn into a competition. The ringleader of this event was my great-grandfather Arnold. He too loved corn on the cob, and he turned this joy into a game. To win, you just had to eat the most.

At age six, I was all in. I remember working my way row by row through the yellow and white kernels, keeping pace with this little old man sitting across the table from me. How a man in his nineties managed to gnaw through seven ears of corn with a gleeful six-year-old, I'll never know!

I can't recall all of the details of the scene, but what I remember most was his presence. He sat at the head of the dining room table and led four generations of his family in making a meal into a memorable contest. His competitive spirit and love of life were infectious.

I only shared about a decade of time on earth with my great-grandfather, but he had an incredible impact on all of his descendants. At the turn of the century, Arnold Bjork went to work full-time for an upholsterer in Detroit when he was just fifteen years old. His own father had died, and as the eldest child, he had to earn money to take care of the rest of his family. When he was let go from that company at age forty, he took all that he had learned, cashed out his stocks, and started his own fabric business: the Upholstery Supply Company. This is the business that my father entered when he was a young man, and it supported Arnold's very large extended family for decades.

But Arnold didn't just build a business for his family. He was also very intentional about teaching them to live a good life. He wrote a list of his best advice to share with his children and grandchildren.

This advice was passed down to me as well. On my wedding day, my dad gave me a framed print of "Arnold's Advice" to hang in my new home. This was my family's legacy, the words we were all meant to do our best to live by. This wisdom shaped our family, generation by generation, and in giving it to me that day, my dad was also passing the torch so that I could light the way for my own children some day.

SHARING ADVICE
ACROSS GENERATIONS

Maybe it's genetic, and maybe it's just been passed down through traditions and routines, but my family is very organized. So it's no surprise that the advice my great grandfather passed down to his children was carefully divided into six different categories:

- Life: How to develop your personal strengths.

- People: How to work with others.

- Family: How to stay connected to the people you love most.

- Saving: How to build and guard your wealth.

- Giving: How to contribute to the good of the world.

- Time: How to manage your most valuable asset.

Over his long life, my great-grandfather developed several rules for living in each of these categories. Each one is carefully distilled into just one crystal-clear sentence, so they are easy to remember—and easy to share. He repeated his advice often to his children and his grandchildren, and it's not hard to draw a line connecting his sage advice to the lessons my dad taught us in our own out-loud family sayings and family laws.

For starters, great-grandfather Arnold was very clear about the importance of being frugal and having the discipline to save the first 20 percent of your income in his rules. The fact that he dedicated a category of life advice to savings shows just how important managing his finances was to him: he believed it was part of the foundation to living a good life. He passed this philosophy down to my dad, who turned the advice into very specific Dad's Class lessons.

This is not to say that my dad just repeated the same advice that my great-grandfather developed. On the contrary, that advice evolved over time, with each generation taking what they found most meaningful, updating specifics for the world they lived in, and leaving behind that which no longer served them. For example, my dad distilled Arnold's six categories of advice into his more streamlined "Three Keys to Life":

- Positive attitude

- People skills

- Passive income

Arnold's commitments to family and building strong connections with others are directly reflected in our out-loud family sayings and family laws. This is where my parents put their ideas into words about how we should treat other people, and these values are directly descended from what they were taught by their own parents. Most people learn their most basic life values from their family, but I'm left to marvel at how my great-grandfather and then my dad took the time to spell their values out in words. I have my great-grandfather's words hanging on my living room wall, and I have my dad's advice written down in a spiral-bound notebook.

This is an incredible treasury of wisdom passed down through the generations, and I am so blessed to have it in such a tangible form. One hundred years ago, my great grandfather began working to care for his family, and he never stopped. His wisdom was earned over the course of a long life, and he was intentional about sharing it with the rest of us. This is an incredible gift, and one that I will one day pass down to my children with the same clear intent: to raise independent, resourceful children who are prepared to succeed in life.

THE FOURTH GENERATION

One hundred years ago, my great-grandfather began his workday before the sun was up. He would drink two cups of plain hot water for breakfast, put on his suit and tie, and drive himself to his office in a city buzzing with industry.

When he sat down at the desk in his office, he would first read the daily sales report and talk to anyone he needed to touch base with for the day. He also spent his morning writing to senators and stockbrokers, people he had nurtured strong relationships with over the course of many years.

After lunch with a group of a dozen members of his old boys' network, great-grandfather Arnold would wrap up some paperwork at the office and come home to sit down in his favorite chair. With his pants button undone and a brandy in hand, he would relax until seven o'clock. This was family dinner time, an unbreakable date where immediate and often extended family would gather around the dining room table for conversation and connection.

Fast-forward to today, and on the surface, my life looks totally different. If I'm feeling ambitious, I'll wake up around six a.m. and hit the gym or do a workout at home before having lemon water for breakfast. Because I work from home, I rarely have a need for a suit and will happily remain casual all day.

There's no secretary or receptionist to greet me, and certainly no one to hand me a cup of coffee. I just open my laptop and get started on my work, which is almost all done online. Sometimes I meet with strong women and amazing men to brainstorm and collaborate; sometimes I work on my own to implement new ideas. The day takes whatever shape I choose to give it, and I run my business with my phone and my notebook, so I can do it anywhere.

After work I have dinner with my husband or maybe a friend, and we settle in for an evening together. That might be spent streaming the latest must-see TV or—in a pre-pandemic world—going out to enjoy restaurants and other events. I also have the freedom to travel and explore the world when I want to, since I've built my life around opportunities that my great-grandfather couldn't have even imagined when he was my age.

Clearly, technology has drastically changed what work and family life look like, but a lot of the basics of Arnold's Advice still resonate. While he wanted us to write to our mothers once per week, I'm happy to text my mom throughout the week to share little jokes and things that I'm thinking about. While my great-grandfather spoke to his stockbroker daily to track his investments, I can fire up an app to deal with every aspect of my finances. While Arnold wrote letters—complete with old-fashioned carbon copies for his records!—to foster connections and build his network; I can shoot an email and CC anyone with the touch of a button.

Technology changes, but values last. It's how you adapt and develop them to fit your own life that matters.

PAIGE'S WISDOM

In writing this book, I wanted to share the lessons that my dad taught me as a child. The specifics of Dad's Class covered important topics about earning, saving, and spending as well as advice for leading a meaningful, value-driven life.

But as I began to dig into my old notebooks and memories, I realized that the structure provided by the lessons was just as important as the content of Dad's Class itself. The fact that my parents spent the time to put their values and lessons into writing and built our daily, weekly, and monthly routines around these tenets revealed just how thoughtful and intentional they were about passing down their philosophy of life to us.

I also realized that they were working in the context of the lessons they had learned from their own parents, and that had been passed down for generations before. Understanding the lineage of my family's teaching drove home the idea that life is cyclical—and it's my turn.

I'm becoming a parent, and that means it's time to shift away from being the student and into the role of the teacher. I'm the one who now needs to get intentional about what I believe and how I want to pass it on to my children.

But I'll share what I'm thinking so far. These ideas have evolved from my family's and my experience, and will continue to evolve based on my own growth:

- Gratitude Attitude: When you wake up each morning, you get to choose how you will face the day. Will you put on a sad face or a happy face? Choosing a positive attitude lets you engage the world with excitement and energy, so this first choice empowers you to live the life you really want.

- World Education: Everything in life is done with other people, so you have to learn to treat them the way they want to be treated and to engage them in productive, caring ways. To do this, you need to honor your commitments to foster trust, and you need to identify and respect people's talents to work with them in the most productive ways. It's also important to be a true "student of the world" to learn new languages, open your mind to other cultures, and seek to understand.

- Intentional Experiences: You only get one life to live, so be sure to spend that precious time in the way that is most meaningful to you—not chained to a job you don't like but need for the paycheck. Making money without having to work for someone else, whether through real estate, stocks, or starting your own business, is the one of the keys to freedom. Passive income gives you back your time to spend as you see fit, so you can do more with your life than just labor.

These ideas have evolved pretty directly from my dad's "Three Keys to Life" listed earlier in this chapter, and it's easy to see the influence of my great-grandfather as well. As I pass them on to my own children, I will focus on the aspects of each that resonate most with me. My Mom's Class lessons will probably have more to do with exploring talents and abilities when we work on people skills, because that's the work that I do professionally. My passive income lessons will also include ideas about how you can create something of value for others that brings in royalty income. All of these have grown from generations of family lessons. Each generation's lessons built upon the previous generation's wisdom, and the lessons I share are no different. The specifics of the lessons change, but the values remain.

BUILDING A GENERATIONAL
WEALTH OF IDEAS

When you look back at the wisdom of your ancestors for inspiration, you will probably find comfort in the knowledge that your parents and grandparents also struggled with the big questions of how to raise their children to become strong, self-reliant adults. They too wondered how to pass their values down to their children in a way that would be useful in an ever-changing world. As you think about the big questions posed in this book, it's helpful to remember that you don't have to do it alone. Even if you are thousands of miles away from your family, you can still tap into their spirit and their wisdom to guide you.

This is the power of building a generational wealth of ideas. It allows you to take the best of the past and adapt it for the future. You don't have to reinvent the wheel! If your grandmother had a saying you love, use it!

Tapping into generational wisdom also strengthens family bonds. When you're intentional about sharing what you've learned from your family, you are also sharing the stories of your childhood and your ancestors' important moments. Building a living, breathing family history gives your children a strong sense of where they come from and how they fit into the bigger picture.

These stories and lessons will also help your children find their way as unique individuals. You already know all the ways in which you are completely different from your parents, and your children will be comforted and inspired to see how you made your own way—just as they will one day be trying to make their own way. Often we forget that families are made up of individual people with different strengths, but sharing wisdom from many different family members only increases the odds that your children will hear something that really resonates with them. Remember, part of passing on generational wisdom is understanding that your children and grandchildren will modify your lessons to fit their own lives. The more material you can provide, the more raw material they have to work with to craft their own rules to live by.

If you've done the work in earlier chapters to develop your values and have become more intentional about finding ways to teach your most important lessons to your children, you're already well on your way to building generational wisdom. Someone has to start the tradition, and you can feel great about being the one to do it first, just like my great-grandfather Arnold did.

But if you'd like to look back to the past to enhance your work for your own Mom's Class or Dad's Class, you can start by asking your older relatives a few key questions.

1. What are the most important life lessons you would want to share with my children? Why?

2. What life experiences had the most impact on the person you've become? Why?

3. What is your definition of success?

4. How did you find success in your career?

5. What are the most important things to remember about people and relationships?

6. What were some of your favorite family traditions as a child?

7. What do you know now that you wish you knew at age ten? Twenty? Thirty?

8. What's the best advice you've ever received?

If you approach these conversations, you will almost certainly hear things that surprise you. With all families, there's the good, the bad, and the ugly in its history. Just because a family member holds a certain view doesn't mean that you have to accept it or share it with your children. As with all conversations about values, bring your ancestral wisdom to the table to share and discuss with your partner, and decide together what's worthy of passing on to your children, what can be modified, and what can be left in the past.

Finally, consider documenting what you learn. You should definitely write down the answers you get to preserve them. You could create a gift for your children like my dad did for me, or you could add them to your out-loud family sayings and family laws to keep them as a living legacy you act on every day. You might even record the conversations with older family members to create a lasting legacy that preserves their voice and image for future generations.

KEY TAKEAWAYS

In this chapter, we learned that advice passed down through the generations can play an important role in developing family values. When you are intentional about what you pass on to your children, you can strengthen family bonds and reinforce the lessons you most want them to learn.

In the course of a century, the most important values and life lessons didn't change much. Even though my great-grandfather Arnold wouldn't have recognized a world filled with video conferencing and social media, his most important ideas still stand the test of time. Values last, so share them intentionally with your children.

I was so lucky to receive this wisdom from the elders in my life, and Arnold's Advice will always hang in a place of honor where my children can see it. This family treasure shows exactly how great an impact your intentional creation of values and lessons can have on your children's lives.

In my case, Arnold's Advice and my dad's Three Keys to Life have helped make me who I am today: a daughter, an entrepreneur, a wife, a friend, and a mother who has developed some wisdom of her own.

CONCLUSION

If you take one concept away from this book, I hope it's this:

You are your child's first and best teacher. When you get intentional about the lessons you teach, you pass on your values and provide the tools they need to succeed.

Your kids will learn from you no matter what, as they watch what you do and listen to what you say—even when you think they aren't paying attention. When you create a structure to live your values and impart your wisdom, you take control of the narrative and make sure that no learning is left to chance. If you don't do it, who will?

In this book, I've provided a structure for planning and suggestions for the content of these important lessons. Ideally, you will be inspired to start talking to your kids about money and life when they are very young, and continue adding to the conversation as they grow. Here's what this can look like over the course of a childhood:

- Age 2–4: Create—and repeat!—out-loud family sayings.

- Age 4–6: Develop and implement family laws.

- Age 6–8: Design daily, weekly and monthly routines and traditions.

- Age 6–8: Establish a family economy with opportunities to earn, save and spend.

- Age 7–9: Start a family bank to teach hands-on financial lessons.

- Age 7–17: Teach your most important life lessons in Mom's Class or Dad's Class.

- Age 10–18: Bring your children to meetings with the professionals in your life.

- Age 12–18: Provide experiences with companies to develop skills and passions.

What happens if you picked up this book when your kids were over twelve? You can still do so much to intentionally teach them what you most want them to know. Many children will happily join in out-loud family sayings with you throughout elementary school, especially if you make it fun, so don't worry if your kids are older than four when you start. You know your kids best, so feel free to modify these lessons and activities to fit their interests as well as their ages.

Flexibility and resilience in the face of change may be the biggest lessons to learn as a parent—or indeed, as a human being. I got married on January 30, 2020, and almost immediately my husband and I were locked together into a small apartment, our honeymoon period spent in isolation. That wasn't at all what I had envisioned when I walked down the aisle, but the truth is that change is always coming, whether it's a slow evolution or hits you like a freight train. The best we can do is stay flexible and keep building—and rebuilding, when we need to—on the strong foundation of our values.

YOU CAN DO IT

The values and lessons I will pass on to my children have evolved from the ones I was taught in my Dad's Class, and his lessons evolved from the ones first written down by my great-grandfather Arnold. Your lessons will be different from mine, and also from the ones your parents and grandparents taught you.

This is exactly as it should be.

You have the power to teach your children anything you want them to know, and to do it in the way that best suits your family's unique values, dynamics, and passions. You might have to adapt and shift gears when a once-in-a-lifetime pandemic comes along, but you can do it.

That's the power of being intentional about your parenting. When you get clear on what you want to teach and how you want to structure your family life, you create an incredibly solid foundation that makes everything else possible. Your rules and routines will support you when things get crazy, because everyone will know what to do and how to interact with each other. And the connections you foster will keep you anchored together in love when things get hard.

I want to leave you with the first lesson I was taught in our first out-loud family saying: *you can do it.* You can be the parent you've always wanted to be and teach your children everything you want them to know. And you can start today.

All it takes is one intentional step. So ask yourself what one action from this book resonated with you the most. Was it the family economy? Experiences with companies? Daily, weekly, and monthly traditions?

Whatever it was, commit to that one thing, and decide how you can start doing it today. Make the intention and act on it. When you do, you'll be giving your child the greatest gift you can as a parent: a piece of yourself that they will carry with them forever.

ACKNOWLEDGMENTS

Thank you to my amazing ghostwriter, Beth Trach. You understood my voice and intentions and were able to put my words into stories so eloquently. I couldn't have created this book without you.

Thank you to Rikki Jump for being so gung ho when we talked about my book as a legacy piece for my family and a guidebook full of wisdom for others. I'm thankful for your enthusiasm.

Thank you to Tucker Max, who put things so bluntly in his workshops: "Do you want to make some bread, or make your book? Your choice." You convinced me during the pandemic to write *this* book, and for that I am grateful.

Huge gratitude to my ladies in life and in business, Alexa Lord and Colleen Mitchell. Thank you for lifting me up when I need it and giving me great constructive feedback. I trust that you both always have my best intentions in mind when it comes to sharing my voice and heart.

Lots of thanks to my husband Peter, who supports all of my wild endeavors, who always gives me honest feedback and continues to be my rock.

Thank you to my siblings, who have graciously allowed me to write my version of our family's story. I hope you accept this book as it's intended: as another expression of my love for each of you.

To Dad: I am so grateful for the intentional teachings that you have bestowed upon me. Thank you for the incredible *quantity* of time you spent with us kids, which I now understand is exactly what it took to make sure the *quality* time would be remembered forever.

Finally, to Mom: This book is because, for, and to you. I love you more than words can express. Thank you for having Mom's Class every day with us!

ABOUT THE AUTHOR

PAIGE CORNETET is the author of the *Spend-Then* series of financial books for children.

She is a fourth-generation, hands-on business owner and the entrepreneur behind Millennial Guru, a business that bridges generational talent gaps in the workplace.

Paige is a passionate educator, speaker, and team facilitator.

She lives in Grand Rapids, MI, with her husband and new puppy, Brick.

Get in touch at www.mydadsclass.com.